THE
deliberate
DIGITAL
MARKETER

First published in 2017 by Grammar Factory Pty. Ltd.

National Library of Australia Cataloguing-in-Publication entry:

Creator: Dahl, Louisa, author.
Title: The deliberate digital marketer : adopt the framework of high-performing marketers / Louisa Dahl.

ISBN: 9780995445376 (paperback)
9780995445383 (ebook)

Subjects: Internet marketing.
Electronic commerce.
Entrepreneurship.
Success in business.

Printed in Australia by McPhersons Printing
Cover design by Designerbility
Book production and editorial services by Grammar Factory

Disclaimer

THE
deliberate
DIGITAL
MARKETER

Adopt the framework of high-performing marketers

Louisa Dahl

Contents

INTRODUCTION

Success isn't something you achieve by accident, but rather by design.

David H. Murdock

Introduction

Success is no accident

T hroughout nearly twenty years in the digital marketing industry, I've watched as my peers have followed one of two routes. They have either risen through the ranks, establishing themselves as leaders and leveraging exciting opportunities, or they have remained in safe jobs, stalling in progress and avoiding any significant moves.

Which route are you planning on taking?

You've picked up this book which indicates that you are likely a person who wants to be successful in your role, combat overwhelm, achieve results and feel good about your work.

Like me, you're probably interested in understanding what causes one marketer to push forward, to elevate, while another seems to stagnate. You want to understand how to be a leader in the industry.

Over the years I've worked with hundreds of digital marketers. As part of my role, I am constantly looking for marketing leaders who can share their knowledge, learning and success with others in the industry. Through this process, I've seen similarities in the way the successful digital marketers approach their careers. I've identified the consistent qualities successful digital marketers share as being they:

- Are ready to leverage opportunities that come their way
- Stay relevant through continual learning
- Forge excellent relationships with peers and industry experts
- Know how to achieve tangible and consistent results
- Get the best out of the resources around them
- Grow their own reputation in the industry as a thought leader and expert.

I have observed professionals at all stages of their careers and at various levels of achievement, and these six qualities have frequently been visible in people who are performing at the top of their game. Without someone displaying at least three of these qualities, I wouldn't consider them an industry leader who can add value to their peers. What's more, these characteristics are interconnected. You don't develop a good reputation without achieving results. You can't have great results unless you stay relevant and leverage your resources. And you don't move to the top of the career ladder unless you're ready for opportunity and forming the right relationships.

Most important of all, however, is one overarching quality that all of these people possess. They are *deliberate.*

Success is rarely accidental. These high performers have come into their roles and achieved career highlights because they have taken deliberate steps to get the right elements in place. While you might develop one or two of these areas independently, it requires a conscious effort to be able to achieve all of these items and be in a position to propel yourself into the next stage of your career.

That's where this book comes in.

Put yourself in the picture

Do you have a picture in your head of what success looks like in your career? I do. After working with achievers and influencers in the digital marketing industry, I have come to understand their challenges and successes. I have seen and experienced what success looks like. Let me describe it for you.

Picture this:

> You are working in a senior role for a high profile, medium-to-large corporation or agency. Or you are part of the founding team in a start-up. You lead a team that works across key digital marketing strategies and campaigns. Your role is valued within the organisation: it carries a lot of responsibility, but you have great support and adequate resources, and you are in control of all aspects of your role. You achieve good results and leave the office at a reasonable time most days.

> You are across the latest trends, knowing what works and what doesn't, and your experience allows you to make decisions quickly across all areas of digital marketing. You understand the organisation and its objectives and you are driving revenue for the organisation, likely through new channels and potential new offerings. You are working to a plan and are confident in your approach, allocating a proportion of your budget to experiments and trying new tools and techniques.

> People frequently approach you because they want to work with you and be part of what you're doing. You are well-connected and have a great network of peers in the industry. You regularly write articles and speak at events. You get approached about all types of

exciting opportunities from working with the latest platform to collaborating with others on complementary projects.

Does this vision inspire you? Can you picture yourself in a role that you love with a workload that energises rather than stresses you? Would you thrive on having that level of influence in your industry: the status, the recognition, the respect? Can you picture yourself becoming the type of marketer an employer wants on their team, colleagues want to collaborate with and companies want to hire?

If you answer 'yes' to those questions, then you have the vision and passion it takes to go far in your career. But how do you get there?

Becoming the deliberate digital marketer

I have written this book to help you, as a marketer, to do your job well.

This book will show you how to benefit from what high-achieving digital marketing professionals have done before you. It contains a framework that will help you solve the most common problems prevalent in this industry, stay up-to-date, become more efficient with your time and get the results that matter.

This book isn't for those people who want to have a job rather than a career, or for those people who stumbled across this profession and don't plan to progress in it. It is for the marketing professional who wants to take control of their career path and advance to the next level.

One thing this book won't do is to tell you how to *do* digital marketing. There is no tactical know-how included within these covers. I'm not going to teach you how to optimise a website, attract search traffic or run email automation campaigns. I'm assuming that you know how to do the fundamental tasks in your job and that you have some education on this topic, ideally coupled with some real world experience. If you are looking for a book to teach you the marketing or digital basics, this is not the right book for you. However, if you're after a framework to help you take your career trajectory into your own hands, you're in the right place.

The Deliberate Digital Marketer Framework in this book offers six steps, based on the six core qualities I've observed in the standout performers of our industry. These six steps will show you how to:

- Tap into your motivation and find a vision so that you can cultivate your career readiness

- Maintain relevance through the discipline of continual learning

- Add value in order to generate great relationships and maintain strong connections

- Form key habits that will help you to maximise your results

- Leverage your resources of time, team and techniques

- Learn the most effective and authentic ways to develop your own reputation.

This book tells you the things that I wish I had known earlier on in my career. I had eight years of experience as a digital marketer and my own agency, and yet I didn't have a career plan to help me *leverage* my efforts. I had a good role, I had a blog, I had some great clients, I met people through work, but I was too busy 'doing the do' to put my hard work to use in a way that would help me beyond that current project, campaign or client.

After years of observing others and working on myself, I have identified what enabled my own career trajectory to take off, helped me progress with my business and has kept my finger on the pulse of digital marketing for nearly two decades. Now I want to share the techniques that I've learnt so that you too can have a fulfilling career.

Do you want to be a great digital marketer? I believe you can be. It's not about sheer talent. It's not about luck. It's not even about wanting it enough. It's about having a clear and deliberate plan and doing the work to implement it. My framework can take you there. This book is your plan.

chapter one

CULTIVATE
READINESS

To have **more** than you've got, you've got to become more than you **are**.

Jim Rohn

Cultivate Readiness

The digital marketing industry is bursting with opportunity. Are you ready for it?

Our industry is under immense change. Technologies, tools, platforms and methods are changing on an almost daily basis. Automation has had a huge impact on how we approach our tasks and roles. Where and when we work, how we work and who we work with/for will continue to evolve. If there was ever a time to position yourself for career opportunities, this is it.

Digital marketing has come from being in its infancy just twenty years ago to being widely accepted as one of the fastest growing, most valued functions in an organisation. It is responsible for higher and higher proportions of sales, new product offerings, entire divisions of companies and a significant proportion of customer interaction and relationships.

Increasingly, digital marketing is at the forefront of guiding innovation and transformation, and leading competitor advantage in an organisation. With over 100 billion connected devices estimated to be in the ecosystem by 2025, digital as a channel is only going to keep growing.[1] Roles that involve digital channels will continue to expand,

1 http://singularityhub.com/2015/05/11/the-world-in-2025-8-predictions-for-the-next-10-years
   http://www.deloittedigital.ca/cdo-assets/pdf/ca-en-chief-digital-officer.pdf

and it is expected that, in the near future, digital silos will be removed from organisations and digital will become the status quo. What this means is more digital-based roles will be in existence than ever before, presenting opportunity for different focus areas and approaches.

As Deloitte explains in its recent report, 'The Rise of the Chief Digital Officer,' convergence is happening: within organisations, the digital strategy is becoming the corporate strategy. Digital is no longer just a function of marketing; rather, it's becoming the foundation of entirely new ways of doing business.[2]

For those of us working in digital marketing, opportunity is knocking! The question is whether we will be ready to open the door and grasp it with both hands.

The entire Deliberate Digital Marketer Framework is here to help you position yourself for this opportunity, and this first step is about preparing yourself mentally – cultivating career readiness. Being 'career ready' is the essential foundation for anyone who wants to succeed. For people who aren't ready, opportunity will pass them by.

In this chapter we will cover the three core components of being ready. These are motivation, vision and mindset. To be ready for opportunity, you need to stoke your passion and know your drivers. To know which opportunities to take, you should have a clear idea of where you want to end up. And to make the most of the opportunities that come your way, you must have the resilience to learn from mistakes and bounce back from failure.

---

2   http://www.deloittedigital.ca/cdo-assets/pdf/ca-en-chief-digital-officer.pdf

Tap into your 'why'

Why are you in digital? Why are you in marketing?

We all have different stories about how we got here and why we love doing what we do. Some of us started out working in this area because it got our attention in a big way, while others fell into it and developed skills and experience along the way. Whether you've ended up working in this industry through conscious choice or a series of small twists and turns, it is important to review your motivation and passion before taking the next step.

Why is this? Because identifying your drivers and staying connected to your passion will help you do your job well and stay motivated for the long haul.

Simon Sinek is the author of *Start with Why*, a book about how we determine and define our why, or purpose. He believes that uncovering and communicating why we do what we do will help us to feel inspired, allow others to resonate with our ideas and support us on the journey. What's more, knowing why you are in this career and what is important to you will provide clarity and purpose. As Sinek says, 'Working hard for something we don't care about is called stress; working hard for something we love is called passion.'[3]

Me? I'm here because I have a fascination with achievement and influence. I first discovered my interest in marketing when I was at university doing the mandatory subjects in my first year of a business degree. I still remember being in awe when I learnt that car manufacturers tailor the sound of a car door shutting specifically to their target consumers. At that point I realised that so much of what I had

3   https://startwithwhy.com

taken for granted in the products and services I consumed was in fact deliberately designed to appeal to me as part of a target audience. From that moment forward, I became interested in marketing. I wanted to learn more about influencing the ways products and services are designed for, and communicated to, consumers.

As time went on I further refined my interest areas, focusing on the digital industry – an industry I fell into when I started my first job out of university, working for an internet start-up not long before the dotcom bubble burst. Seventeen years later I still identify internet and start-up businesses as the areas that most inspire me. I love the constant variability and the excitement of thinking through and trying new ways of doing things. Through the years I have encountered opportunities for less digitally-oriented roles, such as internal communications and education-based projects, yet I've made conscious decisions along the way not to jump at the first thing offered but instead to follow on my path and to stay highly involved in the areas that interest me most.

What is it that drives *you* to be in digital marketing? Is it the responsibility of having an important role within an organisation? The chance to make a difference to customers and the bottom line? Maybe it's the thrill of the chase for results, revenue and reward. Perhaps like me, you love the variability and the opportunity to think outside the square, or maybe you love being at the cutting edge of marketing techniques.

Whatever it is that got you here and has kept you here, take a moment to tap into it. Articulate it. Write it down. Remember it. It's quite liberating to take a closer look at ourselves and understand our motivations.

Deliberate digital marketers know how to use the drivers within them to stay passionate about their career paths, excited about the work they do and energised enough to continually push forward.

Decide where you're heading

Like everything in life, we can't go very far if we don't know where we're going. Along with staying motivated, a vital part of the readiness process is having a vision in place – a clear idea of where you want your career to take you.

Take a moment to think about the career you want to have. Fast forward ten years, or even twenty years. What role do you want to be in at that stage? Providing you have passion and motivation, I doubt that you would be satisfied with the idea of still being in the same team or in a slightly elevated role. Rather, you want to be a business leader, doing exciting work and feeling successful and fulfilled. Maybe you want to progress to the role of the Chief Digital Officer with a seat at the boardroom table. Perhaps you want to be the CEO or run your own business. Or you could choose to run a team of people doing some amazing, rewarding work in another senior role. You may want to be selected to sit on boards for a digitally led business, or perhaps you have another objective altogether.

And that's great. Don't ever be satisfied with the idea of just improving a little bit.

Have a look at the path taken by Ryan Holiday. At just twenty-four he became the Marketing Director for American Apparel. Career jumps like that don't just happen, especially at such a young age. Ryan didn't follow a conventional path to that role. He made deliberate choices early on, even hard ones that resulted in him leaving college early, because he found a path to take him in the direction that he had already decided to go. Ryan aimed high. He spent time learning under smart, well-respected people he knew would elevate him. It's obvious that Ryan has the fire within, which continually pushes him out of his comfort zone and guides him to take risks and try new things. His vision coupled with his passion has led to much success both in marketing and as an author.

There's freedom at the top

If you want to advance in your career, you must aim high – even if it feels a little overambitious, a little arrogant or a little uncomfortable to do so! You must aim above the mark to hit the mark.[4] It is only through having ambitious aims that you will achieve a degree of autonomy. Aiming high equals freedom. Aiming high equals empowerment. Aiming high equals choice.

When starting a career as a digital marketer, everyone plays a role like a cog in a machine. You are usually performing fairly repetitive tasks and contributing only a small component of a larger output, often without an understanding of the bigger picture. However, when you reach the top of your game you can be of fundamental value to an organisation, providing strategic direction, shaping product development and impacting revenue.

The people in charge are the ones who get to have a choice. They are the ones who get to decide how they work, and ultimately this is something *everyone* wants to be in a position to control. Regardless of whether you want a top-paying role, status, flexibility or lifestyle, the higher your aim, the more likely you will be to have a choice about the role you are in. You don't get a choice if you are simply a cog-in-the-machine marketer doing mundane tasks.

---

4   Wise words from Ralph Waldo Emerson.

If you decide not to make a deliberate decision to head for the top, then you need to think about what the other alternative is. If you don't push forward and position yourself in the industry as a leader, you will not be one of those who progresses. Your skills will become stagnant and you will lose relevance. You'll be stuck doing more repetitive roles and lacking opportunity, and with increased automation and artificial intelligence, you could even find part of your role is no longer required.

How high can you go?

When you aim high, the sky's the limit.

The Chief Digital Officer (CDO) is the top of the line in this industry and this role has been getting increased attention in recent years, with reports suggesting the number of CDOs has been doubling each year. Having a seat at the executive table and as part of the C-Suite is a huge opportunity, and reports say that CDOs are now one of the six highest paid roles in organisations. What's more, CDOs are increasingly informing the transformation and innovation agendas for the CEO.[5] Therefore, if you set your sights on a high-achieving career plan, you now have the option to go all the way to the top. You can rise through the organisation easier than most and you will be in the position of having choice.

Digital marketers are also extremely well-placed to start a business in the online space. I can testify to this: I've started three companies of my own in the last twelve years, and many of the successful online start-ups I've interacted with have benefited from a founder or early team member with a digital marketing background. Startup Muster's

5   http://www.deloittedigital.ca/cdo-assets/pdf/ca-en-chief-digital-officer.pdf
    http://www.deloittedigital.ca/chief-digital-officer

recent report on the start-up industry indicates that thirty-seven per cent of founding teams have marketing skills, and what's more, marketing is the number one skill that founders wish they had in their founding team.[6] This skill set is essential in growing a scalable online business, so if you have an entrepreneurial streak, you will always have opportunities to join the start-up world.

If you have the ambition and the vision, there is a world of opportunity open before you. Hopefully, you are starting to get a sense of where it is *you* would like to fit into the picture.

Set the direction, not the destination

At this point you might be thinking, 'How can I know what kind of role I want to hold in ten years' time when this industry is in such a state of growth and change?' And this is a good question to be asking.

You need to be sure of your direction, but not necessarily your ultimate destination. Digital is such a fast-changing industry that we can expect another decade of major change ahead. The role that digital plays in a business and how digital experts fit into an organisational structure is likely to change significantly in the years ahead. Predicting the exact job you want isn't important: what *is* important is choosing what level you want to work at and the benefits you want to receive, and approaching your career with that outcome in mind. You might not want to be CEO or even CDO, but if you head north, and strive to be the best you can in your role, you can choose to stop at any of the roles on the way to the top. Once you know you're heading for bigger things, you can start taking the small, incremental steps towards that goal on an ongoing basis.

6   https://www.start-upmuster.com/Startup-Muster-2016-Report.pdf

I do have one firm bit of advice, though. If you want to position yourself for whatever unknown opportunities come your way, you need to be a generalist.

Go further as a generalist

Choosing your focus area is an important decision as part of the journey. In this industry we are spoilt for choice. Within digital marketing alone there are over twenty specialty areas. You can choose to be a specialist: someone who is an expert in a particular area, such as content, artificial intelligence, video or social. Or you can choose to be a generalist: someone who has broad understanding, skills and experience across several areas.

While being a subject matter expert allows you to have deep knowledge and experience in a specific area, once you get to the top of your speciality division (which may not be very big) it can become hard to extend your skill set and experience to other areas.

In contrast, being a generalist means you have a good working understanding and some experience in multiple areas. It gives you a good strategic oversight across all activity in your organisation. This is where the value comes in. Once you have a clear view of multiple areas, you can spot ways to improve efficiency, avoid potential issues and, importantly, identify opportunities. You are also able to better decide where to focus your time and budget. With an ever-increasing choice of channel and marketing activity, knowing how to choose what to work on is an important component of a senior digital role. This is where you go from being a functional achiever to adding value to your organisation.

Taking a step from being a subject matter expert to having experience in multiple disciplines is usually necessary in order to continue your journey to the top. Without this link, a deep expert can get pegged working in a set role in a specific type of company and have little option to advance.

Cat Matson, the Chief Digital Officer (CDO) for the City of Brisbane, has a definitive view on where digital marketers need to be positioning themselves. 'Being a generalist allows you to connect the dots and see the opportunity,' she says. 'I strongly advise digital marketers who are shaping their careers to choose the generalist option.'

Looking over Cat's career progress, she is certainly practising what she preaches. She has tonnes of strategic experience, has started her own businesses, was CEO of a digital platform and now is CDO for a major Australian city. Cat is also a Director for an arts organisation, adding to her impressive resume. Cat is indeed a deliberate digital marketer, and her advice is well worth taking on board.

What opportunities do you have to start expanding your own skill set and positioning yourself as a generalist?

Looking back over my career history, I value the breadth I was exposed to. Executions have changed, but in essence many principles remain the same. When I started my digital career in a start-up company seventeen years ago, I got to be hands on in activities such as SEO, copywriting, online advertising, transferring files using FTP, online community management, website updates, email campaigns and customer service. This broad experience was an invaluable platform from which to build my career, and I've been grateful for my working knowledge of tactical execution ever since. It has allowed me to holistically write a digital strategy, direct implementation across all tactics, scope and oversee website developments, do needs analysis and be able to troubleshoot and think outside the box when experimenting.

The options available to you will largely depend on the size of the digital team at the company you work. The smaller the team, the more likely you are to be wearing varied hats, and the larger the team, the more chance of delivering in a specialty area. You definitely need a mix of big- and small-team experience in your portfolio, so think carefully about the options available to you right now and consider how you can work towards being a generalist.

If you are in a more specialist role currently, there is plenty that you can do. Start by talking to your manager about how you can expand your skill set within your current position, and choose to take a broader role in your next position.

Having a vision for your career is important and it is the first step in differentiating a deliberate digital marketer from others who float without a plan. Once you understand your motivation and build a vision of what you want to achieve in your career, you are well-placed to take steps forward to achieve it. If you're not yet sure of where you want to go, I've placed some questions at the end of this chapter to help you form your vision.

Adopt a growth mindset

Do you believe you can grow and improve yourself? That, by making a concerted effort to surround yourself with stimuli, you will continually get better? In recent years, the term 'growth mindset' has become a common way to describe this approach.[7]

Our mindset has a big impact on how we view failure, how much we feel we need to prove ourselves, how adaptable we are and what we do when things don't work out as planned. If we have a fixed mindset, we tend to be fatalistic about our abilities and our outcomes. We believe that we can't learn from our experiences or change in any meaningful way. By contrast, if we have a growth mindset, we believe that intelligence can be developed, that we have capacity to grow and change, and that learning new things will play an integral role in our lives.

Carol Dweck, a researcher in motivation, has studied how to encourage a growth mindset in both adults and children.[8] Her research demonstrates that much can be achieved when children come to believe they can grow and learn from their mistakes in a positive way based on the effort they put in. In fact, studies have shown that children who are taught that they make mistakes because they are still learning, and who accept the idea that the more they practice, the more their brain continues to grow, do better than kids who are told that they are inherently smart.

Similarly, research has found that adults with a growth mindset are more likely to want to try harder. They don't view success and failure as polar opposites; instead, they take the view that they can benefit

---

7   https://mindsetonline.com

8   https://www.ted.com/talks/carol_dweck_the_power_of_believing_that_you_can_improve/
    transcript?language=en

from the learning process even if the outcome wasn't the one desired. This means that if you view your output in terms of effort rather than assuming it is a fixed ability, you're more likely to try harder and go on to achieve success.

A mindset critical for digital marketers

Obviously, growing our knowledge isn't a new concept. After all, the majority of us have been encouraged to pursue education as a means to a better lifestyle. But with changing times, what this phrase means for me is that learning doesn't stop once tertiary education does.

In the digital marketing industry, a growth mindset is critical to doing your job well. Without adopting a growth mindset you won't try new things, you'll be afraid of failure and you won't take risks. In a fast-moving, constantly evolving industry, a fixed mindset is a big roadblock: if you don't take chances, you won't take steps forward and you'll be left implementing less-effective solutions with antiquated methods. In addition to this, you'll be defensive of your methods and less open to input.

Innovation is part of the fabric of digital marketing. It is well-accepted that marketing managers should be attributing a small percentage of budgets to trying new things – it's how growth is encouraged within the constraints of corporate life.

We can take inspiration from a company like Google, which had the growth intent when it implemented its 'twenty per cent' time rule. Back in 2004, as a start-up encouraging innovation, employees were encouraged to spend twenty per cent of their time on non-core projects. Some very important Google projects such as Google News, Gmail and AdSense supposedly came out of this innovation-focused environment. While 'twenty per cent time' is no longer utilised in that original format at Google, many other companies including Hootsuite, Apple and Atlassian have worked from similar innovation policies, particularly for engineering and development teams.

As the line between innovation and digital continues to blur, digital marketers can draw on the intent of these concepts as we allocate time and budget to try new and innovative approaches.

Failure + persistence = growth

All digital marketers need to adopt a growth mindset. You need to be thirsty for knowledge and eager to get to that next level. More than that though, you need to be willing to try and to fail in your attempts. Failure is something we all have to get comfortable with.

Again we can look to the start-up industry, which has adopted failure as a badge of honour rather than something to be ashamed of. In the tech start-up hub of the world, Silicon Valley, it has been suggested that founders who have failed in the past are more likely to receive investment from venture capitalists. Being willing to fail shows a willingness to try.

Failure gives us a chance to improve, to try again and to do better next time. Some people go as far as to call failure a feature. Thomas Edison, who invented the light bulb after thousands of attempts, looked upon his experiences not as failure, but as success in proving what *doesn't* work. He famously commented on his experience, 'Genius is one per cent inspiration and ninety-nine per cent perspiration.'

This is the mindset that digital marketers need to adopt: an approach to trying and experimenting that becomes part of regular activity.

This is not to say that huge proportions of the budget should be set on tests that may not get results, but continually trying new things, refining and then testing again, needs to be embraced as the norm.

The ability to fail fast is also vital to the process. No one wants a huge project that has had large amounts of time and money on it to fail. It's important when you are trying new things to only risk what you can afford to lose. Fail lean and fail quick. Be ready to iterate and keep iterating until you find something that sticks.

Adopting a growth mindset

Not sure whether you have a growth mindset? Guess what? It can be acquired.

Individuals, as well as organisations, can take steps to adopt a growth mindset and frame their approach around it. We have complete control over what we think about and that is the first step to embrace this mindset.

Over time, I've learnt that it's okay to fail. Keeping this thought in the back of my head has given me more confidence to try new things and know that I can cope with the outcome if it doesn't go the way I hope the first time. This confidence has helped me try new things in smaller everyday decisions — testing a new campaign idea, hiring a new staff member or trying a new technology — as well as big career moves like launching an internet start-up business. I suggest starting with small decisions that are just outside of your comfort zone; as you develop a growth mindset, you can expand your approach.

Business owner Saga Briggs talks about twenty-five ways to develop a growth mindset.[9] Here are five of my favourite that I recommend trying:

1. *View challenges as opportunities.* Each challenge gives you a new chance to improve.

2. *Acknowledge and embrace imperfections.* Don't hide from your weaknesses; acknowledge them and do something about it.

3. *Try different learning tactics.* Everyone learns differently, so find the way that works best for you.

4. *Make a new goal for every goal accomplished.* Keep creating new goals to stay stimulated and interested in continual learning.

5. *Use the word 'yet'.* If you haven't mastered it 'yet' it simply means you are still working on it.

If you take a growth mindset with you as you progress with the rest of the Deliberate Digital Marketer Framework, and indeed the whole of your life, you will have every chance of reaching the ambitious visions you set for yourself.

9   http://www.opencolleges.edu.au/informed/features/develop-a-growth-mindset

Let's do this

By now you understand that having a successful digital marketing career isn't something that will just happen to you. It's something that you need to work towards, just as many before you have done.

The rewards for working hard *on* your career as well as *in* your career are plentiful, and regardless of what your motivation is, there will ultimately be a benefit for you that makes sense to pursue.

One of my favourite sayings is 'discomfort precedes victory'. Following the rest of the framework that I outline in this book will give you the characteristics you require to become a high-achieving digital marketer – but it won't be easy and it won't be fast. Careers aren't built in a day.

If it were easy, everyone would do it. But I can tell you now, they won't. They don't. More than half of your peers won't even try – they won't pick up a book like this, they won't work on themselves and they won't grow.

You have the opportunity right now to be one of the few who does the hard work and reaps the rewards. You've already stepped up to the plate and made the choice that you want to be deliberate about your career. And once you have tapped into your motivation, defined your vision and reviewed any fear of failing, you'll be on your way.

YOUR DELIBERATE ACTIONS

Now it's time to take a deliberate look at how you approach your career.

- Take a moment to stop and reconnect with why you are in digital marketing and what you like about it. Make a list of at least five reasons – these will help to guide you in your decisions and planning.

- Think about where you want to be in your career in five years, ten years, and twenty years. Consider the areas and roles you want to be in and the direction you want to take. While it is likely that roles will change over time, based on today's information, write down two roles that you would like to be in for each of those stages.

- Consider your experience to date and your current role. Are you a generalist or a specialist? Think about whether you need to expand your skill set and experience in order to broaden your options. What additional experience could you benefit from?

For a deeper look at developing a growth mindset, go to http://www.opencolleges.edu.au/informed/features/develop-a-growth-mindset

Take your time over your answers, as they will form the foundations of your career plan that you'll build on throughout the rest of this book.

chapter two

MAINTAIN RELEVANCE

Change is the end result of all true learning.

Leo Buscaglia

Maintain Relevance

Every digital marketer knows how important it is to stay up-to-date within a fast-changing industry. We've seen how quickly the tools, platforms, products and our customers are changing. We've had glimpses into what's ahead with artificial intelligence, virtual reality and new technologies. And we know how vital it is for us to stay relevant in order to do our jobs well. Maintaining relevance is one of the key strategies in becoming a deliberate digital marketer. The best in the business know how to stay relevant.

The power of relevance

In previous generations, work-related learning ended after school or college. Due to the nature of the repetitive tasks, what you learnt in your youth was enough to get a good job and progress in your role. Following that, the on-the-job learning and experience was typically enough for you to keep that job, achieve marginal improvements to your pay and gain slight elevations to your role throughout your career.

By contrast, as a digital marketer it is not unusual for your role to vary from one day to the next and involve a wide variety of tasks. In addition to this, there are teams of people working to continually modify and improve the very tools you use on a daily basis, meaning that any of them can change at any time. Technology is developing at a rate so fast that some jobs are heading into a future of automation and bots. In a tech-dominated industry, ongoing learning is a necessity to simply remain capable of doing your job.

Relevance comes with the territory

The techniques that I used as a digital marketer even ten years ago had similar theory to the way things are done now, but a significantly different implementation process. While many of the core marketing concepts around customer targeting, usability, appealing to customers and delivering high customer service holds true over the decades, the skills, tools and implementation methods are evolving on a daily basis.

If you are a search engine marketer and you don't embrace the information available about updates to the search engine algorithms or read other people's experiences on how to best adapt your optimisation, within a small amount of time your existing skills will become obsolete. If you continue doing your job the way you have always done it, you could actually be doing a disservice to your customers and your company. Imagine the actual cost to organisations for individuals who don't keep learning on the job.

You only have to look at the rise of social media as a platform to see an example of swift change in the digital marketing industry. Facebook launched to the general public in 2006 and ten years later it has become one of the most popular paid media channels used by digital marketers. Even this channel has undergone significant changes over this period: organic reach for businesses was initially strong and now the platform is primarily pay to play, business tools that were non-existent in the beginning are now constantly developing, and audience targeting is now so widely used that at the time of printing over 11.5 million website pages of advice exist on the topic.

Knowledge is power

Beyond retaining customers, being a relevant digital marketer can reap another awesome benefit: it allows you to be a subject matter expert. In a digital marketing role, you are expected to be the one with good general knowledge of the industry and an opinion on how the latest changes can affect the business you are working for.

Are you capable of providing an intelligent answer when the CEO questions whether one digital marketing platform is more or less effective than another? What about if you are asked your views on virtual reality and its relevance to consumer marketing, or how you see drones impacting ecommerce delivery? Would you be comfortable in communicating the value of digital techniques to stakeholders?

Jeremiah Andrick, the Executive Director of Ecommerce Virtual Reality at HTC, makes a conscious effort to stay relevant by making time to read and record industry data. He has a collection of notes, articles and industry reports that he keeps on areas he is interested in. Recently his CEO had asked him for information on the industry-average cart close rate on a certain type of behaviour. Due to his efforts to maintain relevance, he didn't need to commission research or spend hours looking for an answer. He already had the information on hand and could answer the question on the spot. This not only saved Jeremiah time but also meant he could answer with the confidence expected of a digital leader in a senior role.

Being relevant is a vital step in being good at your job. Coupled with knowledge and experience, it will also make you a force to be reckoned with in your workplace. Given all of this, it's clear that we digital marketers need a strategy to keep abreast of industry changes so that we can implement the latest, most effective methods of attracting, retaining and communicating with customers.

The continual learner

The only way digital marketers can gain the knowledge necessary to keep abreast of the high level of industry change is through continual learning. Continual learning involves making a commitment to frequently review and upgrade your skills. This does not necessarily mean adding new skill sets, but at a minimum it should mean keeping your current skills fresh.

Learning equals relevance. Regardless of the stage that you are at in your digital marketing career journey, if you are passionate about your role you will make ongoing learning a constant part of your life. As Gandhi famously said, 'Learn as if you were to live forever.'

Embracing learning as a way of life once again requires a measure of planning and, you guessed it, being deliberate. To learn effectively, you need to:

- Pinpoint your knowledge gaps
- Identify the right learning resources for you
- Implement your new knowledge.

Let's look at those now.

Pinpoint your knowledge gaps

In order to focus on the right things, you need to be aware of your shortcomings. What do you need to work on?

Ask yourself, 'How can I improve?' Think about the things you know you should be doing and look for areas where you are blocked by fear or unknowns.

We are often aware of our weaknesses, even on a subconscious level, so take the time to stop for a moment and acknowledge your gaps. You may not have a tactical skills gap, but you might need to work on business development skills, understanding the dollars, pitching or getting corporate buy-in. Identify the missing skills that you need to get to the next level and focus on developing these.

If you're not sure what skills you need to work on, start by considering these questions:

1. Are there any areas of your job where you consistently look to others to give you input or advice?

2. What tasks make you nervous? Which ones do you avoid doing? Think about whether additional knowledge could improve your motivation.

3. What areas do your peers and manager say you need to improve on? (If you don't know, ask them!)

4. If you look at job ads for a future role, what skill sets don't you yet have?

Identify the right learning resources

Once you've identified your areas for growth, the next step is to find the right resources to address them. Below, I go through the major options for digital marketers and give you some of my tips for how to make the most of them.

- **COURSES**
  Doing a formal course or in-person class is one of the most direct and effective methods to develop hands-on skills in a new area. In-person courses are often run through industry associations,

expert companies or specific learning organisations. When selecting a course, choose one that is pitched at your experience level.
You might need to look for a master class or advanced class to get
the outcomes you desire. And if you can't find a course that suits,
reach out to someone who is an expert in the area and ask them if
you can pay them to spend a few hours teaching you on the topic.

- **ONLINE PUBLICATIONS**
  Online magazines, blogs, infographics and reports provide the
  latest information around how marketers are achieving results.
  If you are not already doing it, take the time to subscribe to publications and blogs that share information and techniques that
  can keep your knowledge fresh. My favourite publications in this
  space are TechCrunch, Marketing Mag, the WPCurve blog, Ok-
  Dork Blog, CMO, Product Hunt and LinkedIn Pulse, but there are
  also many individual specialists who are learning out loud and
  sharing their experiences.

- **ONLINE LEARNING**
  Online courses can be useful if you want to focus on an area for
  a while and revisit some of the basics. The challenge is finding
  the course with the right topic, quality and level for your circumstances. If you choose learning of this nature, there is usually a
  requirement to do work over an ongoing period of time, so you
  will need to allocate time for this option. Unfortunately, online
  courses (especially free and cheap ones) have a high sign-up rate
  and a low completion rate, so try and make a commitment to following through before you start.

- **WEBINARS**
  Webinars can suit people who take a more visual approach to
  learning, and they sometimes allow more interaction between the

host and the student. They are usually free, but often run by organisations that ultimately are trying to sell you something – the webinars are a step in their acquisition funnel. Be aware of the real-time element: for webinars, you need to either be in the same time zone, or be happy to get out of bed at 2.00 am in order to participate. The benefit of real-time learning, however, is that there is often an opportunity for audience interaction, so you may get to ask questions via voice or through text.

- **EVENTS**
  There are many different styles of events, ranging from networking only, presentations, panels or conferences, and the learning opportunity will vary depending on which style of event you attend. Those focusing on a specific digital marketing topic will give you the most chance to improve your knowledge, learn from other's experiences and stay up-to-date. Put some thought into choosing events to attend and also allow time before and after the event to prepare and wrap up. If you don't take the time to consolidate your learnings into accessible notes and action steps, the ideas quickly disappear.

- **INDUSTRY REPORTS**
  Reports can be either free or paid, and your role and requirements will determine what the best access option is for you. If you're looking for a place to start, try trendwatching.com, a site that provides reports about what's coming up in the industry. Large firms like Deloitte often release information relevant to the industry, or companies like eMarketer or Forrester do specific research that look at everything from device usage to advertising budgets. Most of these reports won't provide direction on specific methods and techniques, but they will give you a guide to compare your results and strategic priorities against.

- **PODCASTS**

  Podcasts are an increasingly popular information source and can be useful for keeping up-to-date. They are also the only learning method listed here that can be done while you are multitasking, be it driving, exercising or ironing! Podcasts are conversations, often interviews and sometimes thought pieces. If you're not sure where to start with podcasts, search for Gary Vaynerchuk, Noah Kagan or Seth Godin. Some start-up-related podcasts also feature very talented founders who are generous with the digital marketing insights they share. My favourites are Marketing School with Neil Patel and Eric Siu, The Marketing Book Podcast, The Digital Week Podcast, The GaryVee Audio Experience, Noah Kagan Presents, The Tim Ferris Show and Social Media Marketing.

- **BOOKS**

  Although books will not be the most up-to-date reference point when it comes to trends and industry changes, they can't be left off this list, as they are one of the richest resources available. I recommend that you incorporate time to read into your week. If reading isn't your thing you can always get the same information through an audio book. If you haven't read the following books, they are relevant to any marketer and I highly recommend taking a look:

  - Any book by Seth Godin
  - *Start With Why* by Simon Sinek
  - *The Lean Startup* by Eric Ries
  - *The 4-Hour Work Week* by Tim Ferris
  - *Ask* by Ryan Levesque.

As you can see, staying relevant as a digital marketer has never involved so much choice. So how do you know which sources and resources to trust? You need to develop a trust scale.

My trust scale is usually determined by looking at a combination of depth of knowledge plus amount of experience. These are the vital determinants in whether someone has something you can learn from. Depth of knowledge is important, as it's impossible to become an expert in any area overnight. Spending time developing knowledge allows a professional to move with the trends, to trial different techniques, to discover what works and to refine and optimise. The amount of experience is just as important, as typically what works for one business will not work for another in a cookie-cutter way. You don't become an expert by implementing a successful solution for just one business. The true expert has made it work many times over across different businesses, audiences and products.

Therefore, when selecting resources to learn from, look for experts who have multiple years of experience in their field *and* experience across more than one organisation.

Implement your knowledge effectively

When done right, continual learning should not just be about being taught something. It's also about determining how to apply that information in your role. True learning requires knowledge transfer *plus* implementation for it to work.

So you've identified your knowledge gaps and chosen the learning resources to help you fill them. Now, how do you ensure that you actually, well, *learn*?

Iterate and improve

I can't stress this enough: simply getting your hands dirty and trying out your newfound knowledge in your own context is fundamental to being a continual learner. Taking new information and applying it to your unique circumstances and then making incremental improvements is the best way to learn, and the best way to maintain relevance as a digital marketer.

In a moment we will look at some other methods a digital marketer can use to support ongoing learning, however actual implementation is best done by iteration and small improvements.

We often expect others to have all the answers for us. Sometimes I see people attend an event and then be disappointed that they weren't handed an implementation plan on a platter. They want a plan of the exact steps they can implement in order to get specific results. But this industry doesn't work like that. There is no one size that fits all. Iteration is about taking one or two ideas from others and combining it with your specific situation to find an outcome that works for you. We are fortunate that as digital marketers our ideas can be tested with relatively small budgets and time invested, and there is detailed measurement available to allow for easy optimisation.

I was at an event recently on the topic of Growth Hacking and one of the speakers mentioned how using an asterisk will usually compel the reader to read the asterisk note further down the page. Another speaker mentioned in passing the importance of social proof when trying to win customers. I combined and adapted these two concepts to trial the idea of using a 'P.S.' in certain emails to reference some testimonials from past partners. The engagement with the first audience I tried this with was instantly improved and yet a second audience didn't give the same lift. It required further iterations before I was able to find the right combination of wording and placement to get an improved response. Adapting my learnings to my circumstance, setting up a measurable test and then persevering with different adaptations until I got the desired outcome allowed me to get tangible results for my efforts.

If you're trialling a new idea for the first time, follow the steps below to make sure you are set up to iterate and improve as part of your process:

1. Define your goals. What outcome do you want to achieve?

2. Decide how you will measure outcomes and achieve goal conversions.

3. Setup one or more tests, ensuring that you only change one variable per test.

4. Run your initial test/s.

5. Check performance against results. What improvements could you make?

6. Continue until you reach the desired outcome.

Sometimes we find ourselves in positions where we are unable to adapt and iterate as much as we'd like due to budget, technology constraints or time. In these situations, we're fortunate to be able to find out what hundreds of other marketers have done and to learn from their experiences. There are many successful marketers who take the time to learn out loud: they decide to explore a topic and then they provide intricate details on what they found out and how they applied it to their business.

Noah Kagan and his team are a great example of this, and have provided step-by-step guides to everything from email marketing psychology to staying organised. You can check out Noah's blogs, Ok Dork and Sumo.com, to get some valuable insights into his own trial-and-error learning. Remember, however, that one perspective is usually not enough, and that implementation using incremental improvements is still going to be the best way to find out how the methods will best work in your situation.

We can also learn from the failures of others and adjust our own testing approach. There are many examples of products that flopped or services that weren't tested and missed vital customer requirements. In recent years, large organisations have set up labs with a view of testing innovative ideas and refining them prior to launch. Organisations like LEGO consider many ideas a month in their labs through a robust process of prototyping, testing and iterating. Only a fraction of these ideas actually see the light of day and when they do, the whole team is confident that the product will be popular with the target market, as they have already done the work, received the customer input and made the necessary changes to ensure there is a good fit.

You might not have a lab at your disposal to test your activity, but you can learn from the processes implemented by organisations to test and iterate.

Alongside trying things out for yourself, there are some other helpful practices that will support your efforts to maintain relevance. Let's take a look at those now.

Schedule your learning time

The hardest thing about routinely doing any task in your life is finding time and making it a priority. In the modern culture of 'being busy', attention is the ultimate commodity – and time is something we never have enough of. Many professionals are in a state of overwhelm: long hours are the norm, schedules are already loaded and it can be particularly hard to make time to do new activities.

But it can be done, and the first step is to consider your ongoing learning as an investment. You need to invest in yourself and in your future, because staying relevant is part of your job. It is an expectation from your employer and from your industry. Try not to think of the time you spend learning as a cost, but rather as an essential part of building a valuable asset. You are the asset, and the return should easily offset your investment.

The second step is to schedule regular learning time into your weekly timetable. Allocating time in your calendar is the only way to really commit to ongoing learning, as otherwise your day-to-day activity will take priority. Here are a few ways that I allocate time in my schedule for my learning activities:

- I batch review articles and industry emails. It is much more efficient than reading them one at a time, so I recommend that you do the same: set up a subfolder, direct relevant emails there to remove the distraction of them arriving in your inbox and mark off some time in your calendar each day or week to read and follow up with your online publications.

- Each week I try to make progress in reading a business book so that I'm averaging a book a month, even in the busy times.

- I've allocated time to listen to podcasts when I'm in the car or doing domestic jobs, so I know I can get a few hours of audio in each week.

- I'm currently spending one night a week doing a professional development course.

The third step is to map out your yearly learning trajectory. Many organisations formally assign training budgets to their staff, so be sure to make the most of this. But whether you are allocated a budget for professional development or not, I strongly recommend that you take the time to review what relevant industry events and courses are coming up and to select ones ahead of time that will plug your knowledge gaps or develop your current interest areas. Most events release date information around six months in advance with program details available two to three months out. Make space in your calendar to do some research once a quarter and select which events you need to attend, which courses you should sign up for and which books you might want to read next.

A final note: don't expect this learning to only be done in the time that is paid for by your employer. If this a true interest of yours, you won't mind staying back that extra half an hour, occasionally skipping lunch or doing some weekend reading to invest in this knowledge for yourself and for your future. Some people like to allocate time for learning first thing in the morning; others choose to watch You-Tube instead of TV at night. I am often reading interesting articles, researching new tools or watching YouTube videos and webinars at night instead of (or while) watching TV. Find a time that works for you and your circumstances.

Record your findings

I don't know about you, but I'm an avid note taker. I know that unless I record information in an easy-to-use format, I won't remember the details in the long term. Professional learning is no different. There are four key ways that I now use to keep records of things I learn:

1. **In a notebook**: Nothing beats writing down notes. I use this method most when watching videos, listening to podcasts and in conversations. A study recently showed that taking handwritten notes actually benefits learning.[10]

2. **Electronically**: I most frequently use Evernote to record learnings and note reference material as it's easily searchable.

10 http://journals.sagepub.com/doi/abs/10.1177/0956797614524581

I save links by subject, along with notes and extracts as required. This year I've also started summarising my take-aways from books I've read and storing these in Evernote.

3. **Audio**: I've recently started recording some conversations that I might need to refer to later. I have set up a tool called Call Recorder in Skype and it automatically records calls. This can be handy when I'm doing an interview or preparing for an event and might want to refer to specific wording in the future.

4. **Digital tools**: These can range from open browser tabs (I always have too many!) to a tool like Pocket, or even Facebook where I save articles. I keep resources I want to look at in these locations. Once I've read them, I make notes in one of the other formats.

Regardless of your preferred format, keeping notes will enable you to access key concepts quickly and easily when you need them, and may also help you to join the dots between your learning materials or combine ideas for implementation.

Jeremiah Andrick, Executive Director of Ecommerce Virtual Reality at HTC, mentioned that, in addition to constantly reading and learning from a variety of sources, he makes sure to keep records of important information for later reference. We heard earlier how this was able to benefit him to answer a question from his CEO. His 'ideas book' in Evernote contains screenshots of interesting reports, ideas for messages he wants to convey in presentations, and his own research and thoughts.

Next time you see an interesting report, some industry statistics or an innovative case study, think about how you can keep a record of it for future use.

Join a mastermind group

Businessman and motivational speaker Jim Rohn famously suggested that a person is the sum of the five people they spend the most time with. This is as true professionally as it is personally. Have a think about your own professional relationships. Who are the majority of your work conversations with? Is this the level of conversation that is going to help you to improve, both personally and professionally? If you are not regularly interacting with the types of peers who can help you achieve and elevate, then consider joining a mastermind group.

A mastermind group is a small group of peers who meet regularly to discuss and solve problems, learn from each other and stay accountable. A mastermind group can be a beneficial way to incorporate regular learning in a face-to-face environment.

I've recently joined a mastermind group for business owners and am finding it extremely rewarding. Not only do I have a whole new network of peers, the advice and input I have received in that forum has been immediately helpful in solving challenges. For example, at the last mastermind meeting, I learnt how some of the others in my group had launched a book. They gave me feedback on the ideas I'd researched and shared specific details of what worked for them and what to do once I'd completed writing my book. On the same day, I was addressing a website migration issue and was able to run my ideas and research on solving the problem past another digital expert to get feedback on my planned approach.

As mastermind groups are typically local to your specific area, you can best find out about them by enquiring with your peers and industry contacts or searching online for groups in your city. If you can't find a mastermind group to suit you, you could form your own. This can be as simple as a monthly lunch with five to ten peers who are working across a range of industries and organisations. Alternatively, you could try an online format: form a private group on Facebook with former colleagues where you can ask each other questions and get advice. Whatever format you choose to use, having a strong connection with your peers can be invaluable.

If you opt to start your own mastermind, consider implementing a structure for the group. A regular format for the conversations will add value and ensure that everyone gets a fair turn to both give and get advice. If you need a starting point, take a look at Chris Ducker's notes for organising a mastermind.[11]

Don't be tempted to form a group with only your current peers or your friends. You are going to get the most benefit if the group is comprised of experts, ideally those with more experience than you or experience from a different perspective. Make sure that you can add some benefit to others as well, even if it is simply through the organisation of the group itself. If you are running the group, you will immediately gain credibility by being the connector between attendees.

11 http://www.chrisducker.com/how-to-organize-a-mastermind-session/

Simple, but not easy

As a digital marketer, staying relevant in your career is quite simple –
in theory. In practice, it's something we need to put concerted effort
into. Nothing I've said in this chapter is particularly new, and I'm
sure you've done parts of the items suggested at some point in time.
The key point I want to make about relevance is that it needs to be
an ongoing element if you want to be successful. It is the second step
in The Deliberate Digital Marketer Framework because it underpins
everything that follows. You can't be good at your job unless you remain relevant – but if you're deliberate about maintaining relevance
through continual learning, you'll thrive.

YOUR DELIBERATE ACTIONS

It's time to be deliberate about how you are receiving and acting on information that will keep you up-to-date, relevant and address any gaps in your experience.

- To help you identify your knowledge gaps, find a position description for a future role. Which skill sets do you feel least confident about?

- Which of the listed resources will help you address your knowledge gaps most effectively? Choose at least three ways to learn that cover both the short term and long term.

- Plan how you can regularly come together with other marketers to collectively discuss and solve problems. Who in your network might know about local masterminds?

- Is there a new app, platform or technique you've been meaning to try? Book a space in your calendar and start testing it this week.

If you want a full checklist of all the suggestions made in this chapter, download it from www.deliberatedigitalmarketer.com.

chapter three

BUILD
RELATIONSHIPS

The business of business is relationships.

Robin S. Sharma

Build Relationships

Relationships, contacts, connections, peers, colleagues, mentors, friends: no matter what you call them, having meaningful relationships and being well-connected is one of the six characteristics I've consistently identified in high-performing marketers.

The business of business

Connecting to people around a common work interest is a vital requirement for doing your job well. These relationships can open up the lines of communication, help you to verbalise your ideas, give you opportunities to collaborate, provide feedback and advice, solve problems and point you in the right direction. It is useful to get perspectives from outside of your own industry and company, and when you are well-connected beyond your own workplace you may be able to draw on these relationships to find your next team member, connect to your next partner or secure your next job.

Connecting with other people lets you learn from those who have done it before, those who have chosen different paths and those who see things differently to you. Throughout my career there have been times when I have been consulting or working in my own business that I've worked alone, and it's at those times that I've forced myself to build relationships so that I can maintain perspective. I've found immense value in this and only wish that I'd also put focus on it when I was part of a larger team. When you are part of a team, it's easy to feel that you don't need to push for an additional external perspective, and yet I believe that it's important to challenge groupthink and keep your sources of information and inspiration fresh.

Chances are that you have regular conversations with your colleagues and your suppliers and that from time to time you catch up socially with some people you used to work with. But outside of this scenario, what are you doing to further develop relationships that can help you with your job and career? What relationships have you formed to help you develop and test your thinking? Are you putting forethought and care into building your connections?

When I think about what it looks like to be deliberate about relationships, I think of David Gram, a senior marketer with a great innovative mind and co-founder of Diplomatic Rebels. David recently worked at global empire LEGO, in Denmark, and he has been in several roles across business development, marketing and innovation over the last six years.

When I asked David about his approach to relationship development, he told me how he has proactively joined several different types of groups throughout his career: there was a group that held regular events for its members, a smaller network where individuals with similar backgrounds met seven or eight times a year, and a group that organised one-on-one meetings between matched professionals. These groups followed different formats but each provided benefit for David, giving him industry input and the opportunity to develop mutually beneficial relationships with new connections.

David is an example of a professional marketer who knows the value in relationships and regularly makes an effort to connect with new people. He tries to meet new people at each event he is attending and if they are interesting, he'll follow up with them afterwards to understand their business and areas of expertise. A number of these contacts he has gone on to work with.

David even credits his job at LEGO to the influence of a connection that he made at an event. Several years ago he attended an Innovation Council event and reached out to a speaker, who was from LEGO, after his presentation. The two of them went on to connect and stayed in touch following that one interaction at the event. Twelve months later when a job came up at LEGO, David reached out to his connection. As luck would have it, this person had a great relationship with the hiring manager on that role and David ended up getting the job!

I am not implying that a connection alone can get you a senior role in a highly respected company like LEGO. David got this particular job on his own merits: organisations like LEGO have stringent recruitment processes in place, and no amount of relationship or connection will replace sufficient industry experience and credibility. However, relationships can pave the way for great opportunities. Having a connection that could vouch for him in this instance was undoubtedly helpful in David's case.

I've also found myself in similar situations where connections have paid off for me. Twice I have created new businesses with former colleagues. On another two occasions I have been offered a new role after I received an introduction from an existing contact. Regularly, a conversation with an existing contact results in them being able to refer a connection to a supplier or another contact I need. All the people I have interviewed to contribute to this book have been connections that I've made through work and stayed in touch with, who now have been willing to share their stories to contribute to this project.

Connections lead to opportunities. They help you to expand your relevance, improve your results, focus your resources and build your reputation. But it's how you go about forming and nurturing relationships that matters.

Forming connections

Focusing your limited time on forming the right relationships is important. No one wants to be involved in unproductive meetings or calls, or to be continually adding value to people who don't give back.

First, have a think about what you want to get from your professional connections. Do you want to be better connected with suppliers or with potential employees? Do you want to build relationships with peers so that you can develop your knowledge and have a wider network to strategise with? Perhaps you want to have more options when it comes to partners or job prospects. Maybe you are looking for someone who can become an informal mentor. When you know what sorts of connections are most important to you right now, you will be able to focus your energies more wisely.

Second, seek out people with whom you can forge an authentic connection. Many business relationships are built around not just a suitable product, service or skill set, but also a genuine connection with the contact point. Take the time to find people who you connect with. Perhaps they have similar experiences to you, whether in work history, skill set or view of the world. Even families and kids can be a talking point in common. Do your research, find your similarities and use these to connect. However, you should always consider the appropriate level of connection for your situation. If you are a junior marketer, you will have more success connecting with mid- to senior-level professionals rather than heading straight to the CMO. Consider not only the value you want from a connection, but also the value you can offer them.

Third, find people who also approach work with a growth mindset. I find the most valuable long-term connections come from people who have a similar mindset to me. They may be in very different roles and industries, but if they are committed to growing, sharing and learning, then there will be mutual benefit. The best connections are made with people who also value the power and opportunity of relationships. Someone with a growth mindset will be interested in not only discussing their problems, but in also hearing about yours. They will be more likely to share their experiences and suggested solutions with you and also want to listen to your opinion. These are the people who will meet you for a coffee or a regular lunch to exchange ideas, challenges and opportunities on a regular basis.

Once you've identified the key relationships you want to focus on, you will start to notice just how many opportunities there are, formal and informal, to form new connections with people who can play an important role in your career journey. It's just a matter of making the most of them.

Below, I've outlined some of the best places and spaces I've found to form new connections with people.

Events

In the same way that events are valuable for learning, they also provide a unique opportunity for connections. Meeting people at events gives you the chance to form an emotional bond, to connect over a common experience or to strike up a conversation on the content you have heard on the day. While you might not always be able to plan who to approach in advance, you already know that you have something in common as you are both at the event and absorbing the knowledge on the day.

This is the hard bit – putting yourself out there to meet new people. I often see clusters of people from the same organisation sticking together for the whole event. They are grateful that they have colleagues attending and spend the entire day together, but it means they don't take the time to talk to anyone else who might be a good connection for them.

Yet I have also seen firsthand the benefits that flow from making new connections at events. At one of the early Interactive Minds events I held, some of the attendees and a speaker met for the first time. Based on that initial meeting and their subsequent follow up, they ended up going into business together. Several years later they sold that business to Twitter. They may never have connected and built something great together had they not met, being willing to share some information about themselves and continued discussions. These are the types of amazing opportunities and connections that can be formed if you are brave enough to put yourself out there.

If talking to new people in this environment doesn't come naturally to you, there are some things you can do to make it easier.

- Request a copy of the attendee list beforehand so that you can decide who you'd most like to meet.

- Consider using a tool like LinkedIn to research people, and be ready to say 'hi' on the day.

- Follow up with an email afterwards or connect with them online and arrange to have a coffee later. This can even be useful for people you didn't get the chance to meet – if you were at the same event, you still have something in common.

Make sure you reach out to the speakers if they are relevant to you too. They are generally available to connect with attendees after their presentations and often share their contact details as part of their involvement. If they are experts in an area you want to know more about, then chances are they are also keen to meet others in the industry and will welcome your interest. You have the advantage of knowing a lot about them once you have seen them speak, so let me encourage you to go ahead and be one of those people who lingers after a session. While no longer mandatory, I personally find business cards are useful for these situations. Business cards makes you more memorable, and they also make it easier for your new contact to find your details than if you exchange details online after the fact.

The other way you can use events is to reach out to new contacts you have recently made and see if they would like to attend an event with you. Depending on the relationship potential, you may invite them as your guest, or you could simply invite them to meet you at an event that might be of mutual interest, or ask them if they are planning on attending too. Growing your knowledge together at an event will build the connection much faster than otherwise.

Follow-up is the key to making lasting relationship connections through events. You might meet people on the day and have a great chat, but if you don't follow through, then you are missing an opportunity.

Sophie Paulin, who spoke at an event I ran a few years ago, recently told me that as a result of that event she made a connection with another speaker, Lisa Messenger, who runs the Collective Hub. These two speakers stayed in touch for months afterwards. Sophie ended up moving interstate and now, nearly two years on, has gone to work with Lisa at Collective Hub. You never know where a connection may take you.

Social media

As marketers, you're likely using social media as an engagement and audience communication tool, but it is also a great way to connect with relevant people on a professional basis.

Personally, I find that LinkedIn is one of the most valuable online relationship tools that exists. I use LinkedIn all the time to find and re-search speakers for my events. In recent years I have also used LinkedIn to meet and connect with people where I can see potential synergies.

A word of warning though – LinkedIn is used by many people as a shortcut to developing relationships, and as such is prone to a lot of spam. For this reason, I rarely actually connect with people using LinkedIn as the first step. Instead, I use LinkedIn to research and find the right person, and then do my initial communication with them *outside* of LinkedIn, usually via email, sometimes on social media. Once we have made contact, I will connect with them on LinkedIn to save them as part of my network. This method gets much better cut through, stands out from the spam and is a lot more flexible. Once you have connected with someone outside of LinkedIn, whether through email, social media or in real life, you are more likely to have your connection accepted.

Twitter has also been useful for me in building relationships with peers. Depending on your industry and interests you may be able to use Instagram, Snapchat or Facebook too. Find out if the person you want to connect with is active on any of the core social media channels, or has a blog or records videos, and reach out to them on their channel of choice. This is a good way to get cut through and to slowly build a relationship.

My advice for using social platforms is this: don't start with a formal introduction, and definitely don't start with a request. Rather, comment on someone's blog post, share their video, re-tweet them or reply to their recent comment. Spend a little bit of time understanding them and their content so that you can build a more genuine relationship.

Email

Email is an effective channel you can use to contact almost anyone. Email can be a personal, genuine and trackable form of communication, and if used properly is an important tool in building relationships.

My biggest tip is to show a genuine interest in your email recipient. I have received far too many emails in which the sender has only talked about themselves and their service offering. Such emails have very little relevance to me, and they always go straight to the trash. If you can include a compliment, send through a relevant article or give them a link to something they may be interested in, you will build a stronger connection. Then, when you do eventually make a request, you are likely to get a better response.

I frequently use emails to make initial contact. It enables me to reach the person I want to communicate with directly. Personal emails are also increasingly trackable using tools such as Hubspot's sales notifications, which automatically tells me when my emails are opened and when links are clicked. It takes the guesswork out of knowing if your email was received. There are also tools available to help you to find an individual's email address. If you're not sure, start with first name.lastname@company.com, or take a look at tools like hunter.io and email-checker.net.

Sending positive feedback via email is an excellent way to connect. For example, you may have just listened to a podcast that resonated with you – why not email the guest or host and tell them? Better yet, tell them how you were able to apply their information to your own circumstance and share your outcome. People always respond well to compliments and simple interactions like this can lay a great foundation for a future relationship. Your feedback may end up being used as a testimonial or it might simply be a stepping stone in building a strong relationship. Make sure you follow through and stay in touch on a regular basis.

Referrals and testimonials

I can't talk about relationships without mentioning referrals and testimonials. Referrals can be proactive, where you ask an existing connection for an introduction, or casual, when you are recommended to a third party because you can potentially add value. We all know how much we value a recommendation from a friend when looking for something we want to buy, and the same applies with professional connections.

Think outside the box about how you might be able to use referrals to expand your network: a supplier might introduce you to one of their clients, a colleague who spoke at an event might introduce you for future opportunities, a connection might connect you to a hiring manager or a peer might recommend their supplier. Depending on your role, testimonials from a client, a colleague or a manager can also be a useful way to validate the value you add.

As nice as it is to have spontaneous referrals made by your connections, in order to take a deliberate approach to your networking, in most situations you will have to request an introduction or that a testimonial be provided. This is where learning to ask comes into it.

Learning to ask

What do you do once you've found the right people to focus your energies on and figured out how to connect with them?

You learn to ask.

I'm a big believer that in order to take an extraordinary path of achievement, we need help from others along the way. This help can be from peers, your company, your broader network or even from strangers. There are many people who can easily give us an advantage, help us to stand out or provide a leg-up.

Often we are too scared to ask for what we want, or we think that asking won't get us the outcome we desire. We are shy or embarrassed about asking and worry that there is no benefit to others. Whether we are asking for a day off, a pay rise or more budget, or even when we are pitching a collaboration opportunity, it can seem like a huge, daunting task to ask.

But it actually takes very little effort to ask and often the answer is just the one we want. Even if the answer isn't the desired one, asking a question rarely has significant negative consequences. In fact, the worst-case scenario is often only the embarrassment of rejection or sometimes receiving no response at all.

So why don't we ask for more? Studies have shown that people underestimate, by as much as fifty per cent, the likelihood that others would agree to a direct request for help.[12] We don't think that people will provide help, yet it is human nature to want to help others. Help seekers also underestimate the social costs of someone refusing their request. Once you ask for help, it's very hard for the other person to say no. Armed with this knowledge, maybe you will feel more confident about asking in the future.

I'm constantly reminded of how the simple act of asking can reap rewards. I run a digital marketing conference for over 600 people each year. We want to be able to offer our VIP guests a little something extra in their delegate packs, but we don't typically have the budget for additional items. Last year I had the idea of contacting my two favourite magazines, one a marketing magazine and one an entrepreneurial magazine, to ask about providing me with some free copies of their magazines to distribute to selected delegates on the day.

But I really didn't want to ask. I put it off, purely because asking is hard. I left it about as late as I could before we needed to pack the delegate bags. Eventually, I reached out at the last minute to both magazines and asked them for some copies. And guess what? They both said yes. One of them asked us to pay a nominal amount for postage, but that was it. Each magazine provided enough copies so that we could distribute them to our VIP delegates. Not only was asking the question simple in the end, but I had achieved the desired outcome within twenty-four hours.

Just as I procrastinated over this task, I have seen people deliberate over things for days – even weeks. They have a great idea that they

12 Reference: http://dx.doi.org/10.1037/0022-3514.95.1.128
  http://www.spring.org.uk/2008/07/ask-for-help-people-twice-as-likely-to.php

want to implement, but they need to ask a third party to be involved. Then they get scared. They don't want to get a no, so they spend time having meetings about it, considering alternative options and generally procrastinating. The thing is, once they realise they don't have anything to lose and ask the question, they generally will get a fast answer and can then move forward (whatever the response). Asking for something can be as quick as five minutes. Thinking about asking can absorb weeks of time and oodles of energy, not to mention the risk of losing momentum.

Remember, though, that there is an art to asking well. When you are asking for something, it's all in how you make the other party feel. When I wanted the magazines for my conference, I didn't just put in a one-sided request. I told the magazines about the alignment of our audiences and why the delegates would be interested in reading their publications. I effectively sold these magazines on the benefits of being involved, plus I told them how much I personally enjoy their publication. A compliment goes a long way.

Not only does asking for something help you to achieve your outcomes, but it also demonstrates to others how you can collaborate with third parties to achieve mutual benefit. Make it a deliberate choice and regular occurrence to ask for things – you'll be surprised at how far this can take you.

Adding value

There's another side to learning to ask, and it's learning to *give*.

The number one rule to developing and nurturing relationships is to add value. You need to give in order to grow. This doesn't just make sense for sales people, but it is useful in any type of relationship. You have to demonstrate your value, and the best way to do this is to provide value. Not only will the person you are helping look at you in a favourable light after the interaction, but you'll be more memorable and they will be more inclined to return the favour.

There are many ways that you can add value to others. I've mentioned some of these before when we've spoken about making connections. These are some of my favourites:

- Introduce a contact to someone they may discover a synergy with, regardless of whether it poses a direct benefit to you.

- Share an interesting article, report or event with a contact you think will be interested.

- Respond to a content creator about the article or social media post they've written.

- Spread the word for someone when they're hiring by sharing links to their job information via social media channels.

Choose to be a person that helps others to connect the dots if you see an opportunity. I frequently get asked to recommend digital marketing consultants who can help businesses with a specific need, such as content creation or running a campaign. I always refer the quality contacts I have. In return, these people are always the first to offer when I need help spreading the word about an event. Adding value and giving is super easy and the returns come back over and over again.

Keeping in touch

I won't need to tell you that the most value will be gained from a relationship when you stay in contact. Long-term relationships are both more genuine and more beneficial than short-term connections. These are the people who will refer you more and have you top of mind. They are the ones you can ask the tough questions of and turn to for advice.

However, this won't happen without regular contact and interaction, and a genuine interest in that person and what they do. I have several tips for nurturing long-term connections.

First, be persistent without being pushy. You need to be sensitive to the dynamics of each relationship. Contacts you are forming will ideally start with a logical link or connection, like work industry or family. Once you receive a response back from the person, which could be as simple as a reply email or an acknowledgement on your blog comment, your relationship has started. From here, you should build on the connection. If the communication is repeatedly one-sided, however, then you need to know when to take the hint and move on, or perhaps give it a break and try again in six months' time.

Second, be creative in your attempts to connect. Relationships that follow from a face-to-face meeting are likely to be stronger than those you develop virtually. That's no reason to shy away from developing online connections, but any relationship will deepen more if you add an 'offline' element at some point. What's more, the relationship will become easier as the number of communication instances increase. The more frequently you interact, and the greater variety of channels these interactions take place across, the more likely a genuine relationship will result.

Third, be patient with the process. Relationships can take a long time to develop any depth. I have several professional relationships I've been developing for ten or more years. When we first met, we were peers at similar levels in our roles. Fast-forward to today and these people are heading up Digital or eCommerce at big brands, or running agencies or their own businesses, and they are all extremely well-connected.

Finally, be open to how a relationship could evolve. As you seek to build your relationships you may have particular outcomes in view, but it helps to keep an open mind. Sometimes a relationship will not provide what you thought you wanted, but may take you in unexpected directions instead.

In 2015 I received an email from a managing director of a local digital agency who was interested in sponsorship options for my events. We had never met, but we had connected on LinkedIn a few years prior. That email resulted in a phone call to discuss the opportunity and a proposal being sent. I spotted her at a conference a few weeks later and introduced myself. The path from here followed a fairly typical business development cycle where I tried to add as much value as possible. I followed up my proposal and we met at her office. I invited her to attend an event I was running so that she could see what it was like and I referred another contact of mine who I thought might be an option for a role this director was recruiting for. At this point we discovered we had a mutual contact who was sponsoring my events, and a subsequent positive conversation with the third party further strengthened the relationship.

This contact never did end up sponsoring us – she had been unable to get to one of our events and had a lot going on in her business. However, things were not meant to end there. A month later another mutual connection brought us together and, with a team of others, we spent a few months evaluating and strategising a new business idea.

We continue to stay in touch throughout these various interactions and beyond, and now I'm proud to call her a friend. We even had a barbeque with our families together and I really value the conversations we have.

While it doesn't often happen that a business introduction can lead to a friendship, this example demonstrates how a variety of interactions, mutual contacts and having things in common can lead to a deep relationship that I have no doubt will continue to be mutually rewarding for years to come.

Whatever your role in digital marketing, relationships are an accelerator for growth. Marketers are well-positioned to be able to find and connect with the people we need to be around so that we can both add and gain value. What's more, if we nurture connections and learn to ask for what we need at the right time, these relationships are an important stepping stone in becoming a deliberate digital marketer.

YOUR DELIBERATE ACTIONS

It's time to be deliberate about how you develop and nurture professional relationships.

- Determine what relationships you would find valuable right now. Do you need people to share knowledge and strategise with, people to explore partnership opportunities with, more referral partners, a mentor or potential job connections?

- Do an audit of your current connections. Draw it up in a mind map or make an Excel spreadsheet. You'll be amazed by who you know. Doing this can also help to identify any gaps you have.

- Consider what value you can offer to other people. Is it other network connections, a shared focus on staying relevant, a report or insight you can offer or the engagement you'll provide? Write these down so you remember to draw on them when making new connections.

- Make a plan for how you will reach out and connect with new people on a regular basis. What channels will you use, how many people will you connect with each month? Time always goes faster than we anticipate, so decide how often you'll touch base with people and put it in your calendar or to-do list.

chapter four

MAXIMISE
RESULTS

The results you achieve will be in direct proportion to the effort you apply.

Denis Waitley

Maximise Results

Results mean everything in the digital marketing business. We all know it. Digital marketers like ourselves are all employed to produce results. Not just any results, but meaningful, positive results that add value to the organisation.

And let's be honest – getting great results is a real boost. Every motivated professional wants to showcase their effectiveness with fantastic outcomes at work. Achieving high results gives you job satisfaction, allows you to be valued in an organisation and provides a platform from which to advance your career.

But, in the highly measurable, accountable world that is digital marketing, the constant drive for results can also become a large source of stress. It's easy to get a poor result from a social media campaign or to have a less than ideal conversion rate. We worry that we're paying too much for search ads or that our advertising campaign has an engagement rate below industry standard. Our campaigns may perform at a mediocre level unless we go to great lengths to make something unique happen. Results can be just good enough to save the channel from budget cuts, but are not successful enough to be a standout performer. The constant pressure of having so much measurability and transparency on every action can produce significant anxiety.

What's more, accurate results can be hard to measure. There are complex, technical, statistically challenging requirements to get all our digital marketing activities working really well and, unless we've inherited a well-designed and implemented infrastructure, accurate and meaningful measurability will always be a work in progress. We also know that despite the measurability of almost everything online, the details we really want to measure are often murky and require complex attribution analysis or tracking that is not fully available or even understood by all the stakeholders involved.

To sum up: we know that results are vital, but they're also hard to measure and produce lots of anxiety! So, what can we do to improve our chances of producing consistent, career-building results?

It's impossible for me, or for any other author, to tell you from afar how to get consistently awesome results from your digital marketing activities. Even if I gave you the exact digital strategy of a successful promotion, it would not work for you. Every situation is different and there is no set formula or plan that will work for every company or campaign.

Results are so much more than just tactical executions. They flow from having a deep understanding of your role within the broader company objectives and knowing how to set and achieve related goals. While we can't focus on specific marketing tactics in this chapter, we *can* focus on adopting the supporting habits that will turn average outcomes into great results.

Good results don't happen by themselves: they happen in conjunction with clear roles, clear goals and deliberate effort. When you identify these for yourself and implement them with your growth mindset, your results will follow.

Clarify your role: which piece of the puzzle are you?

In a results-focused digital marketing role, it is easy to get caught up in the complexities of our own tasks and lose sight of our role in the bigger picture. Here is a scenario to demonstrate:

Pippa is a search engine marketing specialist, part of the digital team that feeds into the marketing unit at her company. Her focus in the organisation is to manage all the paid search traffic and ensure that the product range appears in search results for relevant keywords. She tweaks her search focus based on information from the product team about which lines are the current priority and when the latest advertising campaign will be in market. One of her main KPIs is to deliver targeted traffic at a cost per click of $3 or less and to ensure that the selected products appear on the first page of search results in Google.

Pippa is dedicated to her role and takes pride in hitting her targets. However, even though she meets weekly with the digital marketing team, Pippa could not tell you what her immediate boss's targets involve. She rarely meets with the head of marketing and doesn't have much understanding of what the overall division is trying to achieve.

What I've just described is a fairly common junior role in an organisation – chances are that you or someone you know has been in a role similar to Pippa. Pippa does a good, consistent job and knows how to achieve the goal set for her. But how likely do you think it is that Pippa can really contribute and make a difference to that organisation?

Unless you have some understanding of your broader team context, you will remain unable to reach your potential. It's like doing a complex jigsaw puzzle and not having the picture to know what you are building. You might be able to snag a few pieces together by luck, but without the broader context and goal to work towards, you're unlikely to achieve the ultimate outcome in any manner of efficiency.

Regardless of your role in an organisation, you need to understand not only the expectations upon you, but also those upon your manager and other team members. You also want to be aware of what the organisation as a whole is trying to achieve. I'm not talking about the mission statement of the company or its broader vision of why it does what it does. I'm talking about understanding your organisation's high-level operational goals and how it is tracking against them.

If you want to achieve meaningful output and be considered for a promotion, taking an interest in the context beyond your own role ticks a number of boxes. It allows you to add value to your colleagues and be a more confident part of the team. It demonstrates your interest and subsequent understanding to your boss. Plus, it allows you to get more valuable outcomes and stay alert for complementary opportunities.

In the scenario of Pippa above, how much more value would she add to her team and employer if she were able to achieve her targets *as well as* keep an eye out for opportunities to contribute to the company goals? She could identify an opportunity to work with a content partner in a new way and end up reducing the need for search advertising on a particular product line, hence saving money and allowing the funds to be distributed elsewhere. She could identify a way to get customers feeling more positive about the brand as soon as they landed on the website from a paid ad. Or perhaps she could help test out some key messages around new product lines using paid search.

Know your company's focus areas

You need access to information that influences your context. While revenue and profits are part of the targets set for companies, in this context I'm talking about understanding the current key focus areas and goals of the business. These could be a growth target or a sales quota: for example, you may work for a company focused on customer service who wants to improve their Net Promoter Score, a measure of customer experience, or one who wants to introduce a number of new product lines or acquire more franchisees.

Ideally, you should also look beyond your own team into cross-organisational team reports and data. This could mean understanding the real costs of delivering a product or service to the customer and the figures for sales by product and location, customer satisfaction, repeat purchases, and so on. How can you understand how an offering can best be marketed if you don't understand what the cost of sales is for that item? If, for example, you worked for a company that sells education, how can you know which online course will generate the most value if you don't know which one is more profitable or how many students are already enrolled? How can you influence the company's NPS score if that target is only known to the customer service team?

How can you find all of this information? Ask your colleagues. Next time you are sitting down with your manager, explain that you'd like to ensure that you are helping him/her to contribute to their goals and KPIs and that you would love to understand more about what they are. Find out if your workplace has a strategic document outlining the digital or marketing strategy for the coming year, and allocate some time to really understand what the document means. If you don't understand why the focus areas were chosen, ask clarifying questions. Also ask about what could impact on these goals being achieved. A manager's role is to ensure that these types of plans are distributed and communicated properly, so don't feel bad in asking for the information you need. Sometimes strategic plans and budgets are agreed on without being adequately communicated to the team, so your manager will likely be happy and impressed that you are asking.

The types of information you should consider familiarising yourself with include:

1. **Product information**: Future development plans or project development, stock levels, pricing strategies, cost of goods sold, sales by range, research plans.

2. **Market information**: Competitor insights, strategic partnership plans, corporate sponsorships.

3. **Customer information**: Number of customers, lifetime value of customers, repeat customers, churn rate, net promoter scores, acquisition targets, retention rates.

4. **Performance information**: Sales figures and percentage changes across product/offerings and geographic area, website traffic, conversion rates by channel, attribution insights, engagement, sales pipeline.

5. **Financial information**: Profitability across different products/lines, future forecasts.

Obviously, the focus areas you need to understand will vary across organisations and for different roles. Use this list as a starting point to find the information that will enable you to have a good grasp of your own context.

What if the picture isn't clear?

There are several problems you can come up against when trying to understand your context better. The first is lack of company transparency.

Unfortunately, not all companies make their focus areas or performance tracking visible, not even to their staff. Often this type of information isn't freely accessible to everyone throughout an organisation. Nonetheless, it will exist, and it's up to you to ask for it.

(Hint: now is a good time to use those asking skills we worked on in the last chapter!)

Meet with the people in operations to ask how you can access timely data to do your job better and get outside of your silo. Often, information is not available simply because no one has asked for it, or it's not the way that this job has been done in the past. If you demonstrate interest and ask the important questions then you'll be more likely to receive the information you need to do your job really well.

If your organisation isn't prepared to give you reasonable access to information on performance and profitability, then I'd be asking why. It doesn't make sense to be withholding information that could help you to do your job better. In this case, you have to ask yourself if that is somewhere you want to work. Without clarity about the context of your role, your performance will be held back. In turn, you will not be highly valued by the organisation and the whole premise of being a deliberate digital marketer will be at risk.

What if I discover something that could be detrimental to my role?

The second problem that can crop up when you start looking at the broader picture is that you may wonder where your own role fits – or even *whether* it fits. It may cross your mind that having insight into key data and contributing to the broader company focus areas could actually be detrimental to your own role. Perhaps you discover that your channel is a low performing channel and that in future budget allocations you may lose out, or maybe you discover that the sales levels can't support the same marketing investment in the long term.

In the example of Pippa, she may realise that there is a way to save money on paid search and that it would be better directing the money into something else that is more effective. However, this realisation may also lead her to think that if she relinquishes some budget, this might reduce the need for her role. Feeling threatened could initially cause her to avoid sharing her insights in order to protect her current position and tasks.

But this is the time to think like a deliberate digital marketer who wants to contribute and be recognised beyond your current role. Would a smart employer recognise your valuable suggestion and leverage your skills in new ways, or get rid of you when you are demonstrating value?

While all teams and managers work differently, we need to have faith that if we contribute to a broader company goal, even if it reduces our own budget or workload, then our contribution will be recognised and appreciated and that any created efficiency will be redirected into an equally valuable activity.

This step could actually provide you with an opportunity to broaden your experience and become the generalist we spoke about earlier rather than the specialist who is threatened by change. In Pippa's case, she could now suggest that she contributes to areas outside of the paid search team, which would give her additional experience and boost her career prospects. Taking the time to consider the implications on your role, and being ready with an answer for how you can continue to add maximum value to the organisation, will put you in good stead should this situation occur.

Setting the right goals for you

Once you're armed with a clear knowledge of where your role fits in the bigger picture of your company's goals, you can start setting clear goals that will help you achieve the right results for both your company, and for you.

If you've read any productivity books, blogs or articles, you'll know about the importance of goal setting. People who set goals are more successful. Studies have shown that students who set their own goals take more responsibility and ownership of their learning.[13] In the same way that setting a deadline forces you to focus and achieve in time for a deadline, committing to a goal and having an actionable plan gives you the best chance at actually achieving it.

George T. Doran coined the term SMART goals in 1981 and it is now a widely accepted framework for goal setting. It involves creating goals that are:

- Specific – detailed and to the point
- Measurable – with a clear yardstick for success

---

13 https://hilt.harvard.edu/files/hilt/files/settinggoals.pdf

- Assignable – someone must be responsible

- Realistic – able to be achieved

- Time bound – set within a clear time frame.

Goals need to be specific. Wes Finley, a marketer with over 15 years experience who works at Facebook, recommends that KPIs are well-defined and strictly segmented for a realistic implementation. For example, you can't have a campaign that is going to successfully achieve reach *and* engagement objectives. Rather, these would need to be two campaigns with separate objectives. Define your tactical objectives up front and put the measurement in place to achieve it, as you can't do the work and then arrange tracking after the fact. It's also important to share relevant KPIs with your third-party partners so that everyone is working towards the same measurable goal.

There needs to be an element of measurability in your goal setting. Tie your goals to tangible business objectives rather than measurements without direct value, such as an impression, a like or a share. Wes recommends that KPIs for online marketing or social marketing should be aligned with KPIs for all marketing, such as a conversion, a sale or a lead. These are all measurable and are the most important elements to focus on.

I set a goal to write this book. It's part of a list with nine other goals that I wrote at the beginning of the year, along with action points on what I needed to do to achieve them. If I hadn't given myself a goal to write this book, complete with a target word count and pressing publishing deadlines, then I likely wouldn't be writing this right now. Tony Robbins said 'setting goals is the first step in turning the invisible into the visible'. If you're reading this book, then this book is perfect proof of that.

Owning your KPIs

When it comes to your workplace, you may have KPIs: key performance indicators set by your boss that form part of your job description and are reviewed on a regular basis.

In many organisations, while this is the intention, it is not the reality. Oftentimes, new team members are brought on and thrown in at the deep end with a batch of overdue, high-priority tasks and without so much as a backward glance at their KPIs. Unfortunately, not having clear KPIs can mean that your role is not clear, which can result in lack of both motivation and productivity.

It is ultimately up to you to make sure that you have the right goals set. What's more, you need to have ownership of those goals. If you need to develop your KPIs, or if you haven't had any results-based goals formally assigned to you, then you will need to take it upon yourself to set some goals to help you achieve in your job.

If you do have KPIs provided by your boss or organisation, give these some consideration to check that these are the only numbers you should be judging your success on. While you should always aim to achieve your set KPIs, it is worth asking the questions: Are these the right goals for me? Are there any other goals I should also be including?

Reviewing and setting your own KPIs

To set your own goals, take the following steps:

1. **Review:** Look at your scope of work and identify the key desired outcomes.

2. **Benchmark:** Do a quick benchmark of current activity/results to determine your starting point.

3. **Budget:** Find out what budget and time you can allocate for achieving your outcome.

4. **Set:** Decide what a reasonable improvement would look like, and set a realistic timeline for achieving it.

5. **Check in:** Talk to your manager (as mentioned earlier) to understand their goals and ensure that the goal you have identified fits into the bigger picture.

Let's say that you've started a new role and don't have measurable goals set, but you do have a position description. Implementing the steps above for this specific role might look like this:

1. **Review:** A key deliverable listed in your position description is to increase newsletter subscribers.

2. **Benchmark:** You check in your email system to see how many newsletter subscribers there are now (8,000), how many emails are being sent out (one a month) and how many new subscribers are being acquired through current activities (none).

3. **Budget:** After checking your budget allocation and asking your manager about allowances, you determine how much you will have to spend on acquiring new subscribers ($10,000 for a campaign) and what rate they have been acquired at in the past (no one knows). By considering your workload, you have determined that you can spend up to two days a week on this campaign in the next eight weeks.

4. **Set:** Based on the information available, together with your knowledge of industry standards and acquisition costs, you calculate that you should be able to acquire 1,500 new subscribers in an eight-week timeframe. This becomes your goal.

5. **Check in:** You talk to your manager and discover that she has a target of increasing website sales by ten per cent a quarter, driven through the newsletter, and you confirm that your goal will contribute significantly to this.

Getting buy-in

Finally, it's up to you to share your goals and get buy-in from your manager, leadership and team. Research shows that you are more likely to achieve a goal you have shared with others.[14] Showing commitment to achieving your goal in front of another person helps to keep you accountable and you are even more likely to accomplish your goals if you provide regular progress reports as you go.

Organise a meeting with your manager and talk through the goals you have identified. It is important at this stage to get alignment with the team as individuals and as a whole. If you are only responsible for acquisition, for example, and another team is responsible for driving traffic, then you may have issues of poor quality traffic not converting well. Creating linkages between team goals is important so that the ultimate outcomes are achieved. If you do find yourself in a situation where goals are not working together, raise the issue with a manager and have a solution ready.

One digital expert who has achieved good alignment with her manager through communicating her own goals clearly is Laura Campbell. She has fifteen years of marketing experience, predominantly with large brands, and currently works at Deloitte. She explained to me how she identifies her own list of KPIs and keeps a spreadsheet so that she can enter results and check her performance regularly. Each quarter she arranges to sit down with her manager to check her progress, report

14 http://www.dominican.edu/dominicannews/study-highlights-strategies-for-achieving-goals

achievements and discuss her next targets and focus areas. Not only does this ensure she achieves her own goals and the company's mission statement, but it means her manager knows what she is working towards and sees her successes.

Incorporating career goals

The goals you set don't just have to be about tactical performance but can also be around other professional items that will impact on how you do your job and your future career. You might be aiming to add more staff to your team that would give you additional capacity to achieve results. Perhaps you have a goal for how much time you are going to spend on managing suppliers to improve your efficiency.

I was talking with a marketer recently who has set a target to do a certain number of speaking engagements in a year, as he believes the process of putting together a presentation provides an opportunity for him to improve his knowledge. Others have shared goals of learning business development skills, or gaining additional skills like graphic design, to assist them in doing their job more efficiently.

I wish that I had been better informed about setting goals early on in my career. I had always assumed that the KPIs my employer gave me were the only metric that I needed to think about, but in reality there was so much more I could have given attention to and focused on to make sure that I was doing a great job. Thankfully, I now regularly set challenging SMART goals for myself as well as my team.

Like any other goals, professional development goals require regular review. Again, Laura Campbell provides us with a great model of planning and forward thinking in this area. As a detail-oriented person who wants to ensure she keeps achieving, Laura has created a one-page dashboard of her key priorities and performance targets. This incorporates not only the KPIs set by the organisation she works for, but also those she has personally identified as being relevant. She keeps the dashboard up-to-date to track progress. Although it is not an obligation of her role to complete this level of reporting, Laura says it is a way for her to ensure she stays focused on her targets, remains aligned with the organisations priorities, adds value to her role and positions herself to achieve her bonus.

Planning of this nature may not come naturally to everyone, but hopefully hearing how other digital marketing experts are approaching their KPIs will inspire you to make it a focus area. Taking a deliberate approach to your goals can apply to projects, to client objectives or to your role as a whole – and in each of these circumstances, a deliberate approach will give you the greatest chance of producing great results.

If you're doing it all, you're doing it wrong

Once you are clear on your KPIs and goals, it's time to review how you are going to structure your activities to achieve them.

Digital marketers can often feel overwhelmed when considering the hundreds of different tasks and tactics available to us. The constantly evolving digital landscape means there are always many options to consider when selecting activities to implement, and one mistake people make is trying to do them all at once. We don't need to be operating on every social media channel, tackling multiple technology implementations and trying every new advance as soon as it is available.

Rather, it is important to get a clear picture of which activities are giving us the most effective results that align with the goals we identified earlier.

I find it helpful to remember the Pareto Principle, which states that eighty per cent of the effects come from twenty per cent of the causes.[15] You may have heard this concept used in other scenarios: eighty per cent of sales come from twenty per cent of customers, eighty per cent of revenue comes from twenty per cent of products or twenty per cent of your time produces eighty per cent of your results.

The point of this principle is that there is an uneven distribution between efforts and outcomes. It may not be a strict eighty/twenty breakdown, and the numbers don't need to add up to 100. The point is that you want to identify the actions that are giving you the most bang for your buck, as well as those actions that are taking up far more time than the results they appear to produce.

If you apply this theory to your results efficiency, then you can ask yourself the question: which of my efforts are driving the bulk of my results to meet my goals? To combat overwhelm, can you focus on that twenty per cent and amplify that activity, rather than trying to do the full 100 per cent of activities you currently make a priority?

To find the twenty per cent, it's useful to do a 'results audit'. It is a bit of an undertaking – yes, it uses valuable time – but you are likely tracking all your results already and you only need to do the additional time tracking occasionally (for example, once a quarter).

15 http://leadershipcoachingblog.com/wp-content/uploads/2012/03/the-80-20-principle-to-achieve-more-with-less-effort1.pdf

For one or two weeks, do the following activities:

1. Keep a list of all the activities you do (use a table similar to the format below). For easy comparison, consider doing one table for each performance outcome you are working on.

2. Take note of how long you are spending on each activity.

3. At the conclusion of your time, look at the results for each activity.

4. Calculate performance by dividing the results by the amount of time invested.

5. Find the items that are producing the highest results. Sometimes this will be an easy calculation (as below) but other times you will have a less tangible outcome and will need to make a decision based on your own feeling of effectiveness.

Website traffic time audit

Activities	Time (weekly)	Results	Performance
Social media	5 hours	5,000 unique visitors	1,000 per hour
Blog articles	15 hours	12,000 unique visitors	800 per hour
Partner content	4 hours	1,000 unique visitors	250 per hour
Email	6 hours	1,000 unique visitors	166 per hour

In the example above, you'll see that there is not an exact eighty/twenty calculation. But what stands out is that the performance of some activities far outweighs others. What you're looking for is the relationship between time spent and the results gained. It is likely that you will discover some activities that are taking a lot of time and yet producing results at a lower rate than other activities, and some that are performing well for comparatively little effort.

You can use this activity at a number of different levels. For example, you might be doing paid search and can drill down to find the twenty per cent of keywords that are driving the eighty per cent of traffic. Or, if social media marketing is one of the tasks you spend a lot of time on, you can compare the platforms you use. Sometimes we need to let go of channels that aren't performing or don't serve another purpose for the business.

However, I know that it isn't always possible to ignore the lower-performing areas. Often we maintain them not for direct returns but for other reasons, such as keeping a channel open to customers, providing information or keeping the boss happy. But if results are ultimately the number one measure of your effectiveness, consider how much time you should be allocating to areas that don't contribute to your KPIs. Perhaps this exercise may even uncover some areas that need to be discussed in terms of their performance priority.

It's likely that these non-performing activities get grouped in with all the other tasks on your plate and they get as much priority as the performing areas. So, this is a reminder to prioritise accordingly and to know that it's okay to scale back your activity. Determine your best-performing areas and focus on them. Double down and work them as hard as you can and make sure they are delivering maximum value.

Once you are sure that you've accelerated the results from those priority areas, you can look at how to add in additional activities. The key is not to attempt to do it all at once. If you are not going to do an activity purposefully, then don't do it at all. It will only take time and effort and deliver stress rather than results.

Having clear goals and knowing exactly what you need to achieve in your role will place you in the best position to be producing strong results in the areas that matter. In turn, this will reduce your stress levels, remove ambiguity, clarify purpose and pave the way for consistently strong performance.

YOUR DELIBERATE ACTIONS

It's time to be deliberate about developing your goals and achieving results to align with them.

- Get clear on your context. What are the KPIs and goals for your manager and your team? What are your broader company goals? If you're not sure about these, who are you going to talk with to find out?

- Review the KPIs you have been given. Can you identify any additional goals to add? Take three of these KPIs and set yourself some SMART goals that relate to them.

- Put some time in your calendar to review your performance on a quarterly or six-monthly basis. You could also schedule in a meeting with your manager so you can discuss these goals and get buy-in.

chapter 5

LEVERAGE
RESOURCES

Focus is a matter of deciding what things you're not going to do.

JOHN CARMACK

Leverage Resources

In the last chapter we looked at having the right goals and selecting which activities to focus on in order to get great results; which leads us directly to considering what resources we can draw upon to help us fulfil our goals.

Resources can refer to the *time* you have available to you, the *techniques* you have at your disposal and the *team* you have around you. As you progress into more senior roles, creating time for the high-level tasks, finding the right productivity techniques and learning how to get the most out of your team will be of great benefit to you, as each of these areas can greatly affect your success. In this chapter I give you some tips to get the most from your resources.

Creating time

We all have the same amount of time – and it's not enough.

I often see digital marketers in a state of overwhelm. In our industry we spend our hours trying out the latest trends that have poked their heads up, juggling hundreds of varied tasks to drive activity and results, managing a team, setting expectations and getting buy-in from others. Most digital marketers feel like they will never get it all done and are stretched way too thinly between all the tasks on their plate.

When I recently surveyed a room of over 100 digital marketers and asked what their biggest work challenge was for the week, 'time' was listed in the top three issues. Specifically, the people I surveyed felt that they did not have enough time to complete the tasks on their plate, prioritise tasks, manage deadlines or plan time to be creative.

Whether you are running a marketing department or focusing on one particular channel or campaign, it is likely you have felt like this at some point. This feeling isn't isolated to our industry or profession, but as digital marketers we operate in a constantly changing environment and there is pressure to keep up with it all. And in one of life's ironies, there is an inverse relationship between time and success: the more successful you are, the more support you can afford and the more time you can get back. Unfortunately, this means that until a certain level of success occurs, you'll continue to feel pushed for time and need to do more on your own.

Despite the challenges, there are habits we can adopt to work smarter and influence the amount of time we allow ourselves to focus on things that matter. Time can become our friend, not our foe. As John F. Kennedy famously quipped, 'We must use time as a tool, not as a crutch.'

Identify your low-value tasks

One way to approach the weekly task breakdown is to categorise your tasks into high- and low-value activities. Analysing what kinds of activities you spend your time on will allow you to become more efficient.

Broadly speaking, your work tasks will fall into two groups:

1. Strategic tasks (high value) that require you to develop a plan and use your particular skill set, connections or thought leadership to be completed. These are often infrequent and don't follow a formula.

2. Repetitive tasks (low value) that can be documented as a process and don't require significant strategy or effort.

By 'low value', I don't necessarily mean 'low performance'. Low-value tasks are often the bread and butter of great campaigns and consistent results. Nearly everyone starts their careers by doing a higher proportion of low-value tasks. Whether it is submitting information to forms, entering content on a website or making repetitive document changes, this is a normal part of learning and gaining experience. However, as you advance in your career, the aim should be to gradually do fewer low-value tasks and shift the larger proportion of your time to high-value tasks – even if this means relinquishing some of your high-performing activities! Yes, that's right: if a high-performing task is easy, repetitive and sucking up too much of your time, it will be worth your while getting it off your plate in order to make more room for high-value, strategic activities and leadership opportunities. Think about what it would be like if you had fewer low-value tasks on your plate and could spend your time on the juicier, more fulfilling tasks.

Regardless of where you work or how big your team is, there are certain low-value tasks that have to be done. When these tasks need to be completed on a recurring basis, it's time to hand them off. Here are some of the low-value tasks you should not be doing once you reach a mid-level role and above:

- Entering website content
- Generating reports

- Submitting forms
- Editing graphics
- Setting up ad campaigns
- Coordinating travel
- Issuing invoices
- Responding to standard customer queries.

These are not one-off tasks: they follow the same processes or routines and need to be done frequently or in large batches.

Pull out your to-do list and take a moment to review it. Highlight the items on there that are low-value tasks. How many of them are there and what will you do about it? What would you spend your time doing if you didn't have these tasks on your plate? It's time to do something about it.

Your main options for dealing with low-value tasks are to delegate, outsource, create processes or automate.

Delegate

Delegating sounds so easy. However, regardless of your employment level, it's easy to get stuck doing low-value tasks on a regular basis. I know this too well. Sometimes it feels quicker to jump in and change an error on the website, raise an invoice or manage a minor customer request myself rather than brief someone else to do it. Logically, I know that these tasks aren't the best use of my time and should be handled by another person in my team. I also know how much better it is for me when I focus on strategic, value-adding tasks.

Why is it so hard to delegate? There are several reasons why we unintentionally create roadblocks for ourselves in delegating work. We can get lazy in briefing the task to another person in the first place, or feel that it will be easier for us to 'just to do it' rather than take time to document a process so that someone else can always do it, because we simply want to get the task crossed off our list and that seems more important than delegating at the time. And sometimes we think that someone else can't possibly do the task as quickly and efficiently as ourselves. But, deep down, we all know that is not the case. Teaching another resource to do low-value, repetitive tasks can take them off your plate forever and give you some valuable time back.

You may be fortunate enough to have a team to delegate these lower value tasks to. If that is the case, there is nothing to stop you. You'll first need to put a case forward to your manager on gaining additional team support. Here is a basic guide to putting your delegation case forward:

1. Calculate how many hours of low-value tasks you are currently completing a week.

2. Calculate your hourly rate.

3. Work out the current value of you doing these tasks (hours x rate).

4. Look at the other team member's hourly rate.

5. Calculate the cost of the team member doing these tasks (hours x rate).

6. Find the saving of the team member doing it instead of you (your cost – team member's cost).

Usually this calculation alone should be enough to convince a manager of the need to remove low-value tasks from your plate. If not, simply look at the opportunity cost of the work you can't get done if you keep doing these tasks. Outlining what is missing or what you could achieve instead will demonstrate how you could better use your time.

An excuse people sometimes use to avoid handing tasks over is that the proposed team member also won't have the capacity to take on the work. It is important to check that assumption. Sometimes we make assumptions about other people's workload that aren't correct, especially if the resource doesn't report to us. Talk to your manager and their manager as your first port of call and see what you can figure out.

Outsource

If you still need additional help, consider exploring the option of a virtual assistant (VA) for your team. More and more companies are starting to invest in virtual team members to complete low-value, repetitive tasks. The idea of outsourcing to a virtual team member has generated a lot of interest, particularly by small business owners and entrepreneurs after bestselling author Tim Ferris wrote about it in *The 4-Hour Work Week*. It has since had a huge uptake as individuals, teams and organisations have adopted outsourced team members.

Taking on a virtual assistant can be as easy as signing up with an organisation that manages virtual assistants. Or you can find an individual through a site like Upwork, which provides a resource similar to an independent contractor. Alternatively, you can engage a company that is providing VA services specifically to the marketing industry.

Depending on which path you take, you'll find that an experienced virtual assistant will cost you as little as US$5 per hour. Keep in mind, however, that you will get what you pay for, so the cheapest option isn't always the best.

A VA can be used not just for low-value marketing and administration tasks but also for personal development tasks and even 'life admin' such as:

- Putting together a resume
- Applying for jobs
- Conducting industry research
- Scheduling speaking engagements.

I have been using a virtual assistant on and off for several years and have had them do everything from work-related research and information collation through to researching children's birthday party options. Virtual assistants give us the option to make the most of the time we have.

If you want the team member to be a true part of your team, you need to shop around for the right fit and establish effective processes for their tasks.

Create processes and use automation

A further option to streamline low-value tasks and to save time is to document efficient processes and embrace basic automation for relevant team communication and tasks.

A process is simply a way to document the most efficient way to complete a task. Its purpose is not only to define the method to be used, but also to allow that task to be easily completed by a new resource as required. A process document can be as simple as listing the steps involved, together with tools, templates and resources to effectively do a task. The initial time investment for writing out clear processes is well worth the return in time saved on briefing people about routine tasks.

Automation can work hand in hand with processes to streamline tasks. This could mean setting up email filters so items you don't need to touch can bypass your inbox. Or you can arrange for automatic reminders between team members as one person completes work that requires another person's input. Automation tools like Zapier can help teams to work efficiently together.

Ronsley Vaz, CEO of audio marketing agency Amplify, uses processes and automation to great advantage in helping his team run more efficiently. Ronsley believes that any time a task is performed more than once, a process should be put in place. This has reduced his team's workload and has led to quality, consistent output. Ronsley puts processes in place for a range of tasks from managing workflow and internal communications to monitoring team satisfaction and hiring new resources. Everything that can be automated is, with a view to streamlining communication and keeping to schedule. For example, as soon as one of his team members saves a new audio file in their folders, another team member is automatically notified to advise them the file is ready. Ronsley's team also report on their capacity each week. If they are flagged as being over capacity for two weeks in a row, a process is put into place to hire a new resource.

If you haven't formed or implemented processes for your work, think about what you are doing on a frequent basis and how you can improve by adding some workflow and automation.

Say no

My final tip for creating time is an oldie but a goldie: learn to say no.

Saying no can be hard – it goes against the grain. Instinctively, we don't want to let other people down. But sometimes, saying no is necessary. We have already discussed that we can't do everything at once or we won't be doing a good job. Saying no is a simple way to create time and to allow you to focus on the things that matter.

Saying no could mean choosing not to explore a new channel when it's not the right time, or deciding against adding a new campaign when it's not aligned with your KPIs. Sometimes it's as simple as saying no to a face-to-face meeting and proposing a phone call instead – this approach alone has often saved me hours. If you know you won't be able to meet a deadline, don't say that you will as it just creates unnecessary pressure.

Even when a straight no won't be possible, you can come up with an alternative solution, change other deliverables or reduce the scope you are promising. We are in control of what we say yes to and there will always be more to do. Sometimes everyone needs to push back.

Time is such a limited resource. It's worth checking regularly that you aren't unintentionally spending it on things that you shouldn't be – performing a time audit and identifying your low-value tasks will help with that. Once you're aware of how your time is distributed, you can create more time for yourself through delegation and outsourcing, process creation and automation and, when necessary, saying no.

Now that we've looked at those, let's turn to some techniques that can improve time management even further.

Embracing techniques

If you are already prioritising your tasks and focusing on the high-value items, there may be ways you can still work smarter. There is no silver bullet here, but I can share some of the time management techniques that I've had success with in the hope that some of these might work for you.

Uni-tasking

We've all tried multitasking. It sounds great, but does it work?

Although we can sometimes feel efficient when we quickly check our email while a form submits or switch tasks when we get a blank on a creative solution, studies have shown that switching tasks is a lot more inefficient than we realised.[16] In fact, it is generally accepted that when we toggle between tasks it can take twenty to thirty minutes to refocus our minds on the task at hand and it can reduce productivity significantly.[17]

Focusing our attention on one thing at a time and completing it before switching gears is a desired skill and a much more efficient approach. As Teri Hockett wrote in an article on quitting multitasking, while it is important to be able to wear many hats, we shouldn't be trying to wear them all at the same time. Allocate a specific amount of time to a task and work without stopping (this is a similar concept to the Pomodoro technique which is explained ahead). Choose the right time of the day to uni-task when you aren't expecting a high number of phone calls or interruptions. And clear your desk so you don't get distracted by papers!

16 https://www.fastcompany.com/944128/worker-interrupted-cost-task-switching
17 http://www.nytimes.com/2013/05/05/opinion/sunday/a-focus-on-distraction.html

If focusing on one thing is something you struggle with, start by turning off your email, social and phone notifications when you need to concentrate. If needed, explore tools available that will stop you from being distracted:

- Install www.freedom.to to block apps and websites
- Try out Google Chrome's productivity extension, StayFocusd
- Take a look at www.rescuetime.com to see how you are spending your time in the first place.

Batch-tasking

Batch-tasking, or batching, is about grouping similar tasks together so that you can do them in one hit.

For example, you might choose to allocate a day a week where you work on strategy and plan your upcoming campaigns, or you may want to spend half a day a week analysing results and planning for the week ahead.

I've heard of content marketers who plan their content pieces on one day, write articles on the next, review and edit on the third day and then publish and promote the content on the fourth. Rather than do each of these tasks every day, which sometimes can be hard to get to, batching them and putting them in your calendar accordingly can be a great way to ensure they get done with maximum efficiency.

Batching can be used both for ongoing tasks, where you schedule batching time every week, or tasks that just need to get done in one hit a few times a year.

I've already described how I batch-read my industry emails on a weekly basis, but I batch a lot of other tasks too. Part of my job involves finding expert digital marketers around the world and connecting with them for mutual benefit. This is certainly a job that I can do one person at a time, but when I actually block out half a day or more in my calendar, get my tools ready and batch the work, everything changes. Not only am I significantly more efficient, but the results occur in batches too. This gives me both a sense of momentum and the buzz of achievement.

The Pomodoro method

When I'm feeling overwhelmed by tasks and my to-do list is looking stressful, I often use the Pomodoro method to make sure I'm achieving in a productive and controlled way. This is a time management technique that involves working uninterrupted for twenty-five minutes (called a Pomodoro), taking a short three- to five-minute break, then doing another twenty-five-minute block. After doing four Pomodoros, you then take a longer break of fifteen to thirty minutes.

Using this method helps me to be realistic with what I can achieve in a day as I plan out in advance which tasks I will do for each Pomodoro. When I use it, I find that I remain focused on the task at hand and am much less prone to distractions.

Do, delegate, dump or defer

Earlier we spoke about how you can manage low-value tasks and some of the recommended concepts should also be considered across your full task list for effective time management. Your tasks can be split into four categories:

1. **Do** the tasks that you should do immediately, as they will likely relate to your goals and drive an outcome.

2. **Delegate** tasks you need to delegate, such as updating content or running a standard report.

3. **Dump** tasks you know are not important and can be removed without action.

4. **Defer** non-urgent tasks that you can set back for an amount of time.

An easy way to use this tactic is to write your to-do list using colour coding. You could use red for tasks that should be delegated to someone else, blue for tasks that you need to do and green for tasks that are a lower priority and can be deferred. If a task needs to be dumped, you can simply cross it out or not write it at all.

This filter can be applied to everything from your email inbox to your to-do list and can help you focus on what matters. It can even apply to your meetings. If you're feeling time poor, simply review your calendar with this lens and rank commitments accordingly.

Tech tools

We are spoilt with a choice of technical tools to use in our work which can help us to be more efficient. Whether it is Trello for tasks or Canva for graphics, tools can help us to collaborate, use templates and short-cut our work. Some of my favourite efficiency tools are:

- **Canva:** I create graphic templates that can easily be reused with new content and don't require a special skill set.

- **Last pass:** I can use different passwords for different sites without having to remember them and I can log in quickly. I can also share passwords with the team as required.

- **Loom (Chrome plugin) or Quicktime:** I use these to take quick snapshots or explanatory videos to share with my team.

- **Voice dictate:** I'm using this more frequently on both my phone and my computer to dictate messages or emails. It's fast, efficient and increasingly accurate.

Now that you are feeling more confident about how to manage your time, let's take a look at how to leverage one of your most important resources – your team.

Forging a team

Career progression frequently comes with increased team management responsibilities. Team members can be a welcome relief and their presence can give us opportunity to do more, but at the same time the increased workload and people management can result in stressful situations for many digital marketers who haven't necessarily had the training or experience in managing a team.

When we come to see our team members as welcome resources rather than additional work or responsibility, we can start to enjoy the synergies of teamwork. There are many resources and processes available to help you to find and manage your team to get maximum results. It is not my intention to duplicate these here. Rather, I'd like to share some of my personal experience and tips, together with insights from other high-performing digital marketers and business leaders, on team management approaches that work.

Look for people with complementary skills

Richard Branson famously said, 'It's all about finding and hiring people better than you.' Create a team that will help you to achieve your objectives and allow you to focus on the tasks where you can each add the most value. Often we hire people like ourselves – people with similar experience and similar skill sets – and we think that bringing them on the team will allow us to offload some of our tasks. The best leaders choose to bring on people who can fill their skills gaps rather than replicating their competencies.

Don't be afraid to hire people with complementary skills to yours and aim to hire people who are even better than you. Several years after I started Interactive Minds I decided to bring on someone to help me manage the events I was running. I had the choice of bringing on a junior who I could train up, or an experienced resource who could take me to the next level. I chose the latter. Now over six years later I'm still grateful for the skills this hire brings to my team and the different focus and attention to detail that they add.

Grow your team through your connections

We've already covered the value of developing meaningful relationships for your career. Here I want to look at relationships through the lens of building a high-performing team. Generating relationships with other people in the industry can be beneficial for your career, but it can also help to fill roles within the company where you work.

In addition to hiring several people I don't know, I have on multiple occasions hired people with whom I've had a previous connection. Over the years I have been involved in recruiting someone I went to university with, two extended family members and another former colleague. I have also recently brought five people into my team and three of those I have known in some capacity for several years.

This doesn't mean showing favouritism. While bringing someone known onto the team can add a level of comfort to the hiring process, having a prior connection with a candidate doesn't mean that they bypass the recruitment process. In fact, having someone you know involved in a recruitment exercise can put additional pressure on all parties. I'm usually more conscious than ever to follow the process and be sure that I recruit based on experience, capability and merit, as I don't want any bias to result in a decision I regret.

Ultimately, using your connections as part of the process can help to open up the talent pool and sometimes will allow you an edge over another employer. If you don't already know the people you want to hire, it's an opportunity to use your network to spread the word. I frequently share available roles with my social media groups and I'm often asked if I know anyone to fill a specific role in other companies. Usually I do refer people and share relevant roles, as this an easy way I can contribute to my relationships.

Credit your team with successes

In this book I talk about building relationships, growing your reputation and achieving results. In nearly all cases, these scenarios require other members of your team to contribute to your success. A capable and empowered team will play a significant role in the success of digital marketing activities, and it is always right to give credit where credit is due.

One of my favourite marketing minds, Seth Godin, says it well when he talks about reflecting credit and embracing blame. As a manager, you should always take responsibility when something your team has implemented does not work out as planned. On the flip side, when success does occur, it is important to give credit to the people who contributed to the outcome and not keep the accolades to yourself. Not only will this approach get the most out of your team, but it will also gain respect from your peers and colleagues.

As marketers we need to encourage an environment of innovation, continual learning and experimentation to get the best results. We want our team to feel comfortable in taking reasonable risks as part of their role and to be free from blame or consequences. Taking this approach will facilitate a culture of innovation and growth in your team.

Hire slow and fire fast

When recruiting new members for your team, my advice is to hire slow and fire fast. This is a lesson that I've learnt the hard way, and sharing my experiences with you might help you, should you find yourself in a similar position.

I've hired for a number of roles over my career and have typically followed a standard recruitment process. While I often get a good feel for a team member through the interview process, I have learnt to value pre-employment cognitive ability and behavioural assessment as well. Finding the candidate who is not only experienced and skilled enough but is also behaviourally suited for the role has led to hiring more autonomous staff. In the few instances where I have not paid attention to the pre-employment test results, I have paid the price with a less-than-capable employee who took a lot more of my time and energy than they should have.

Like many managers, though, I find letting team members go to be one of the harder elements of managing a team. While I am happy with my hiring process, terminating a staff member is something I have not been doing well.

I recently listened to a podcast from Entrepreneurs On Fire (EOFire) that talked about hiring slow and firing fast. Hiring slow involves taking your time in recruiting, building rapport with your prospective employee and making sure they are a good fit for the team's culture and objectives before making a commitment. In contrast, firing should ideally be a quick process. As soon as you have a conscious thought about getting rid of that staff member, you should then follow through and do it fast. This is because your subconscious would have been tossing this idea over for some time before it reaches your conscious mind and therefore when it does, you should do something about it sooner rather than later.

Often, we don't fire fast enough. We tend to think about all the reasons we can't get rid of that person just yet: the busy period is coming up; getting thirty per cent out of them is better than nothing; I don't have time to replace them right now; they need the money. The list goes on and on. I've been caught here more than once, hoping that the person takes feedback on board and improves, or waiting for a more favourable time in the year to let them go. But the outcome is always worse if you give them the benefit of the doubt for too long or make excuses to keep them on.

It's useful to remember that if the situation is not working for you, chances are that it's also not working for the other party. It's best that they leave on mutual terms that you can influence rather than leaving you in the lurch.

This delicate job of hiring and firing staff should, of course, be done not only with due consideration to the employee or contractor but also to comply with HR policies and employment laws. Setting a practice task is a good way to gauge ability and skill levels prior to hiring, and agreeing on a probation period enables a trial period while also having an out clause. Needless to say, check in with your local agency to ensure that any employment activities you undertake fit in with the local laws.

The way we use the resources available to us can play a big role in our outcomes. While some of the techniques covered in this chapter are fairly straightforward, it's about finding the methods that are a good fit for your role, work well within your context and support your plan. A digital marketer who has their time, techniques and team working well for them is in the best position to succeed.

YOUR DELIBERATE ACTIONS

It's time to be deliberate about how you manage your resources:

- Identify the low-value tasks, recurring tasks you are doing. Which of these could you delegate or outsource? Who could take them on instead of you?

- Go through your to-do list and calendar and mark out tasks using the Do/Delegate/Dump/Defer approach.

- Are there opportunities to create processes and automation to improve your efficiency and that of your team?

- Look at how you arrange your time and consider trying out the uni-tasking, batching or Pomodoro method.

- Look at your current team and identify gaps and opportunities. Start thinking now about where you will find the people you need six or twelve months ahead.

chapter 6

ELEVATE
REPUTATION

The results you achieve will be in direct proportion to the effort you apply.

DENIS WAITLEY

Elevate Reputation

Do you know how you are perceived in your industry? Do your peers know and respect you and your work?

Reputation – we all have one. Although it can feel like it's something outside of our control – based on other people's perceptions of us – it's actually up to each one of us to cultivate our own. If you want to be a deliberate digital marketer who is well-positioned for opportunities, then you need to be known and respected as a leader in your field.

For this reason, reputation is the final step in the Deliberate Digital Marketer Framework. It is the last element that we discuss because it requires all of the other elements to be activated in order for you to develop the *right kind* of reputation. Your reputation is built on your success and requires achievement to have already occurred. You need to ensure your skills and knowledge are relevant; you need to be achieving results, have developed relationships and be effective at leveraging your resources. Only then will you be well-placed to capitalise on your reputation.

The idea of doing self-promotion to build your reputation might be outside of your comfort zone, but it isn't as daunting as it sounds. This section will cover some steps that everyone can take to get started.

Why elevate?

Everyone knows that it's beneficial to have a good reputation; I don't need to convince you of the benefits of that.

However, I may need to convince you of the merits of deliberately working to elevate – lift up, enhance, boost – your own reputation.

You see, your reputation is not a passive thing. Yes, it must be built on your prior experience and results; but it is not a mere by-product of these results. It's also something you can actively work on. It's something you can influence and help to grow. You can be deliberate about your reputation.

While being proactive about building your reputation won't necessarily come naturally to you, it is an important part of preparing yourself for opportunities in your career. If you've been used to thinking of your reputation as something largely out of your own control, then you may need a little more convincing that you should actively work on it. I have some good reasons for you right here.

- **IT CONNECTS YOU**
  Taking the time to build your profile in the industry will mean that you become better known among your peers. Then, once you have a recognised profile, you can leverage this to build more connections in the industry. It's certainly easier to form new relationships if people have heard of you and your work, and can see you will bring value to the relationship. These relationships are also more likely to be built on respect. Having a raised profile positions you more directly to receive exciting opportunities to collaborate, give your input, contribute to something bigger or simply meet

some interesting people. The pay-off is access to even more opportunities as a recognised leader.

- **IT DIFFERENTIATES YOU**

   While it's easy to talk about your reputation in the terms of your next career move, that is not all it's about. Yes, being known and respected in the industry will enable you to take progressive career opportunities when the time is right – as you've seen with several of the senior digital professionals that I interviewed for this book. Beyond that, however, your reputation is what differentiates you from the others. It helps you to stand out and be known among your peer group. Having a reputation means that you have taken the time to equip people with the information or proof of your capabilities, and this will allow you to develop more meaningful relationships in a shorter amount of time.

- **IT BENEFITS YOUR EMPLOYER**

   An ideal outcome for a digital marketer building their reputation is that they will also raise the profile of their organisation in the process. When an expert gains publicity, media or industry attention through discussing innovative methods or successful outcomes, their employer can also benefit from the positive attention. The individual has articles published, gets invited to speak at events, is interviewed on topical items and the brand they work on benefits from the mentions and gains a higher profile accordingly.

How to elevate

Hopefully you can now see why elevating your reputation is important, so let's move onto thinking about how to do it. In this section I'll give you some high-level tips on how to boost your reputation, then I'll outline the best tactics you can employ in doing so.

Choose your workplace wisely

Your reputation is built on your experience, and part of planning a deliberate career is making sure you have the experience you need to take the next step. Earlier on we spoke about your decisions around your role and the choice of being a specialist or a generalist. Here, I want to make a mention of being selective about which company you choose to work for.

Make no mistake: you will be affected by the reputation of the company that you work for. If you work for a large, well-known and respected organisation and you do well, you will be able to leverage a brand that is known and loved. If you work for a brand that has a reputation for poor customer service or being controversial, it will be more difficult to step away from that. If you work for a company that is small and relatively unknown, you may need to work harder to get attention.

Think about where you want to work and plan your roles accordingly. If you want to work as Head of Digital Strategy at a fast moving consumer goods (FMCG) company, for example, you will likely need to have experience at other FMCGs prior to reaching that role. Similarly, if you want to work in a senior agency role, other agency experience will be valued.

Choose the people you work for carefully and deliberately and think about how that role will be a stepping stone towards the next.

Speak up!

Newsflash: nobody will know about your work unless *you* tell them.

As you progress in your career, there is a point at which it is extremely valuable for your reputation to precede you. If industry leaders don't know about the work you are doing and the level of results you are achieving, why would they reach out to you with opportunities? Even at an internal level, you need to be able to share your wins in a way that positions you as a valuable employee and key member of the team. Success is contagious and people naturally want to be associated with someone who is doing well.

Keep records

However, you may come across resistance to your efforts. If you have an employer who doesn't support you in your attempts to raise your profile, the best thing you can do is to track and measure the effect yourself so that you can demonstrate the benefit to them.

Earlier I mentioned a friend of mine, Laura, who works for a large consulting firm. Laura regularly speaks at industry events. Initially the company she works for didn't see how her event involvement would be worth the investment of her time. Rather than deciding not to participate at future events based on this feedback, Laura instead started keeping detailed notes on the outcomes from her speaking engagements. When she met people at the events, she recorded it. When people contacted her after the event to follow up with her, she kept notes. When she was offered opportunities as a result of that speaking engagement, it was written down. When new business came in from those connections, she noted that too.

And the results speak for themselves. Speaking does lead to opportunities. From a single event, Laura calculated that ten per cent of the audience contacted her to follow up and this resulted in her meeting with half of them to discuss opportunities. As business development forms part of Laura's role, this is a significant outcome. Once Laura was able to demonstrate these types of results, her speaking commitments were made a higher priority in the organisation she works for.

Put yourself forward

In my role, where I have run nearly 100 events over the last eight years, I'm not only on the lookout for high-achieving digital marketers who can share their experience with their peers, but I'm regularly approached by agencies and providers who want to speak and get their brand in front of our audience. These individuals and companies have realised that participation in events is a great business development tool, establishing them as a thought leader and resulting in new business opportunities.

Wouldn't you also expect, then, that digital marketers across a whole range of positions and companies would be reaching out to build their profiles and speak at events? But have a guess at how many professional marketers, who are not trying to sell a product or service, have approached me for a speaking opportunity in the last year. The answer is less than five.

Very few professional digital marketers are taking the opportunity to grow their profiles and leverage events in a proactive way. Unfortunately, digital marketers aren't maximising this option to boost both themselves and the companies they work for. It's a lost opportunity. Don't wait for it to come to you. Those who make opportunities for themselves will receive the greatest rewards.

Be consistent to be memorable

Building your reputation doesn't happen overnight and requires regular attention and commitment. You might need to speak four times throughout the year, write a weekly article and share frequently on social media in order to build and maintain a profile. Doing just one of these things won't be enough: like all marketing activities, you will need a strategy for how to amplify your actions.

As you are building your reputation, it is important to be both memorable and accessible. You want to be easily remembered so that people can contact you for those future opportunities. You need to be easy to find online, whether through an email address, your blog or personal website or via a social media channel. If you are too hard to contact, people won't bother. If you want the opportunity to be interviewed by an industry magazine or collaborate in an upcoming campaign with a complementary organisation, ensure that people know who you are and how to find you.

Be generous

Your reputation also comes from sharing your experience and know-how with others. We'll talk about how in the next section, but here I want to focus on the importance of sharing generously.

I meet the occasional person who doesn't want to share their knowledge and experience with others, or they don't have permission from the organisation that they work for to share. They are so proud of what they have achieved, and yet petrified that someone else will copy them and emulate the same success. But even if you did share every single detail of a specific campaign or tactic with others, they'll be unlikely to be able to copy it, and if they did, the chances of that one thing leading to success are very minor. It takes more than an example and details of one tiny element of the business to implement something great. It takes a team, a good product, a customer base to resonate with, customer service to support it – I could go on! It takes a whole ecosystem of marketing activities to support the one key element in discussion.

Sharing details about a small piece of the puzzle and being open and transparent in doing so isn't going to jeopardise a business. In fact, being generous with information is more likely to be beneficial in the long run and may bring you totally unexpected opportunities.

Add value

While building authority is about your reputation, it's not all about you. Like the key message I wrote about in the relationships section, reputation is also heavily reliant on adding value to others. You don't want to only talk about yourself, your results and how good you are. You want to benefit others by sharing information that they will be interested in. Think about the key lessons you have learnt, what you have got wrong and why, and what you would do differently next time. Share your newly acquired knowledge and your vision for the future. Teach how others can benefit from your experience. This approach positions you as thought leader in the industry and will instantly give you a step up on your peers.

Finally, when you are looking for opportunities to build your profile, remember that you need to add value at that stage of the process too. Don't just send your bio onto someone and hope that it will be enough to allow you to write for them or speak for them. I can tell you, a bio is rarely enough. Can you bring them some new content, a new audience or a different perspective that will be relevant to their audience? Provide details and be willing to put some thought into it before you approach someone. Always start with how you can benefit them and not just talk about what you want. You will get a much more positive outcome.

It's time to market yourself

There are many ways to share your knowledge, experiences and wisdom with your peers and others in your industry. In most cases, you need to generate content in some form, be it written, video, audio or presentation, in order to demonstrate your leadership and participation.

The key objective is getting your name known and respected in the industry. Some people do this by focusing on a particular topic or two and diving in deep as an expert on this topic. I know one professional who aligned herself with the target audience of the company she worked for to become known as the expert on 'Millennial Marketing'. Alternatively, you can take a more general approach and be knowledgeable across a variety of digital marketing topics. Either approach can work well, but put some thought into it beforehand. Where is your key interest area, what are you most comfortable talking about and where does your wealth of knowledge sit?

This is your chance to market yourself, so approach it as seriously as you would approach any other campaign. This is not a one-off task: it needs a considered plan, some set targets and ongoing activity in order to create and then maintain your industry reputation.

The good news is that it will get easier as you go. Once you do the groundwork, you'll find that things gain momentum. Getting published in one publication gives rise to other publications. Speaking as a guest on one podcast will often result in an invitation to be interviewed on another.

Developing your reputation is effectively a content play and the sooner you approach it professionally, the easier it will be. Remember Jeremiah Andrick and how he saves information he finds valuable for future reference? When I was talking with him, he also mentioned that he had a few presentation decks he was putting together as he went. These weren't for any specific upcoming event, but rather so that he has a content store of information he's passionate about ready to use at short notice for future opportunities. How forward thinking is that?

So where should you start? Here are a few ideas:

- **SOCIAL MEDIA**
  Maintaining an up-to-date online profile is a must have for any deliberate digital marketer. Not only is it vital for building your reputation, but people need to know where to find you and how to contact you. In addition to this, social media provides the opportunity to engage with others via this channel.

- **START A BLOG**
  A digital marketer should be able to create and publish a blog easier than most, so consider if you've got enough to say to create a personal destination for your content and profile. If setting up a blog isn't your thing, another option is to contribute articles to other people's blogs or company blogs as a means of publishing content. If it's your own blog, you will need to work on developing a database or following; tools like LinkedIn Published Posts or Medium can help to get you some reach.

Frequency of content is important, so plan out your topics and series. Once you have a topic you can use a mind map to work out connected subtopics. I have found this a great way to detail all the areas a series of blog posts should cover.

- **WRITE ARTICLES**
  Publications are always looking for articles contributed by industry experts. As long as you are careful not to push sales through this channel and can write something of value to their readership, contributing articles is fairly easy to do. I have written for or contributed to various Australian industry publications like *Marketing Mag, The Australian Financial Review, Anthill Online, Digital Brisbane, B & T, Inside Small Business* and *marketing.com.au*. In most of these cases I reached out to the editor directly. If you manage to establish a regular contribution with publications like these, you could then leverage this exposure to write for global publications.

- **MAKE PRESENTATIONS**
  Presenting at seminars and events is a great way to establish yourself in the industry. Speaking at events can be a longer-term goal as it can take a while between first contact and getting on stage, but once you get a few experiences under your belt it can snowball quickly. If you haven't done many before, start with the smaller Meetup events and enrol in some speaker training so that you are confident on stage. Don't expect to get paid unless you are a headline act at a very expensive event – even then, consider the opportunity more than the dollars. Once you start to get speaking requests, be careful not to say yes to everything. Speaker burnout can happen and it's better to do a bunch of select events a year and have fresh content, rather than do one every week.

- **PARTICIPATE IN PODCASTS**

  Podcasts have grown in influence in recent years and are a great channel to explore. There are plenty of marketing-focused podcasts, so use your networks to see if you can present as a guest on someone else's podcast. You shouldn't need to pay to appear on a podcast, but do think about what you can contribute that's of worth. Starting your own podcast is also worth considering as a means of raising your profile while also developing valuable relationships. Dave Eddy, who has a podcast called The Location Station, says, 'If I was a 20-something year old right now, I would start a podcast interviewing digital marketing experts about all their best tactics and strategies. This is an easy, fun, awesome way to grow a young digital marketer's network and learn directly from the pros! This is exactly what I've done with The Location Station Local Marketing Podcast and it's been the best thing I've ever done. Wish I did it years ago!'

- **ENTER AWARDS**

  In our industry, there are plenty of awards to nominate for. Of course, you literally need to be in it to win it, so choose some awards in advance that would be good for you to enter. If you are selected as a finalist, make sure you announce it!

To be perceived as an industry leader, the bottom line is that you need to create content. The options I've listed above are a great place to start, but there are many creative options to explore. Find the channel that is right for you, whether that be live video, webinars or something new.

Planning pays off

I'm a planner through and through, so it's no surprise that I'm going to say that planning to build your reputation in advance pays off. What's more, you are going to get more momentum and have greater impact if you do more than one of these activities at a time. Perhaps there is a topic or case study that you can build up and re-use across several of these channels. You could develop a deep presentation, write a series of articles around it, be interviewed on a podcast and enter into a suitable industry award. Just as you would in your profession as a digital marketer, try to create content once and re-use many times.

I also recommend having a follow up topic available, so that you've got more than one thought area that you can become a thought leader in through the medium to long term.

Wes Finley, from Facebook, explained to me how he is always building collateral and preparing presentations ready to use when they are needed. He has spoken at several events and recently invested in training to further improve his speaking skills. Wes sees the value in speaking at events as it provides him an opportunity to revisit topics he is interested in and in order to keep his presentation fresh he also takes the time to learn more about the topic area too. He has experienced firsthand how the value of presentations can extend beyond the initial commitment to create new connections and lead to other presentations and opportunities.

Wes demonstrates a very deliberate approach to dedicating time to building his reputation, and this dedication to his career is probably how he ended up working for one of the most desirable employers in the world!

While it may feel like a lot of work, when you make a conscious effort to work on your reputation, most of your work is in preparation for the first opportunity. If you don't then re-use that work to spread the word even further, you're selling yourself short.

I believe you should approach your reputation development in the same way as you would think about putting together a digital campaign. Just as you would use content across many channels, your personal profile content is no different. You know better than most how to do this. Now is the time to get your personal content strategy in place for maximum effect.

YOUR DELIBERATE ACTIONS

It's time to take deliberate steps to build your reputation and market yourself.

- Check that you are accessible and that people can find and contact you easily online. If you're not, make some time in your diary this week to fix your online visibility.

- Write a list of all the topics that you could use to form the basis of a blog post, an article or a presentation. Then do a mind map for each one, listing subtopics and related ideas. It can be daunting at first, but if you keep an open mind, more ideas will come.

- Choose at least three channels to contribute to: a blog, a publication, regular social media contributions, speaking at an event, a podcast interview or entering some industry awards. What steps can you take this month to get started in each area?

CONCLUSION

Implementing The Deliberate Digital Marketer Framework

Continuous effort... is the key to unlocking our potential.

WINSTON CHURCHILL

Conclusion

Implementing The Deliberate Digital Marketer Framework

You've now been introduced to the framework. These six steps will help you to be a better digital marketer, take a deliberate approach to your career and position yourself for exciting opportunities. No one should expect these changes to happen overnight; all good things take time, especially if you want a long-lasting result. Patience and timing is an important part of achievement, however, if you do follow this framework you can expect to see benefit from your efforts sooner.

And, really, it's all about creating space for opportunity: opportunity to do quality work, meet interesting people and be involved with interesting projects. Opportunity to be fulfilled professionally and experience less stress, all while having some fun.

Now it's time to implement. You have invested time reading this book, but unless you take some action as a result, you won't be able to benefit from the knowledge. Absorbing information alone isn't enough – it's what you do with the knowledge that counts. Now is the time to act.

Of course, finding that time is a challenge. Nobody has as much time as they would like to do everything they want to do. Not having time is also a handy excuse when we don't want to push ourselves out of our comfort zone. It would be easy for you to fall back on that now. You could say, 'Yes, I read *The Deliberate Digital Marketer*, but I don't really have time right now to spend on my career. I'm already spending so much time at work.'

I get it. Spending more time on your work might not go down well with you or your partner. It could challenge your idea of a work/life balance and disrupt your ideas about what to put into your career at this stage.

But this book isn't about spending more time working. It's about being *smarter* in how you work, and doing what you need to do to in order to progress. If you make this a priority now and do a little bit of work to set up some good systems, you will ultimately be creating time for yourself down the track.

I'm the classic case of someone who is always stretched for time. But it is a choice, and I have chosen to stretch myself. In the last few months I have chosen to make the time to write this book while working in my own business, growing my business and being a hands-on parent of three kids under ten. Yes, I've had to sacrifice some other aspects of my life (mainly sleep, TV and exercise), but I decided it was a priority and I have treated it as such. I know it won't need this much time forever, but it's part of my professional development and it's worth it.

I hope that you choose to find the time to invest in yourself now too.

Here's some final inspiration and motivation to help keep you on track.

Find your inspiration

There are three things you can put into place today that will help you to follow through with the Deliberate Digital Marketer Framework.

1. Become a fan

We know that imitation is the greatest form of flattery and when you're planning your career approach, it's a good place to start. Take a look at the top performers in the industry right now. Is there someone you have a lot of respect for, but don't know and haven't met? If no one comes to mind, check out a marketing publication and look for one of their recent top lists. Lists like 'the most innovative people in marketing' get published every year, and you can use a list like this to find someone who inspires you. I recommend finding someone in your own country as a starting point.

Once you have found someone you consider to be a successful digital marketer, then become their fan. Follow them online, subscribe to their updates, read their blog, search for articles they have written or been mentioned in. Study their journey, their rise and their success. Look at what they did and how they did it. Once you know a bit about them, you may even be able to connect with them.

As I'm writing this, there is one person in Australia who immediately comes to mind and fits my picture of a successful marketer. This man has had amazing career progression, which can be seen purely at a surface level in his resume. He started off in a variety of marketing roles and then spent over a decade working with a well-known computer company, at which point 'online' became part of his job title. He then moved to a large bank, and it was during this tenure I first heard of him. It seemed to be a time when he worked particularly hard to demonstrate thought leadership and raise his profile through public speaking and publications. I love that his LinkedIn profile for this role says, 'I'm determined to make a difference at *Company* as a marketing and online leader.'

Over the last number of years, this expert has spoken frequently at industry events, kept an active personal blog and contributed regularly on social media. One of his recent blog posts is a list of the newsletters that he uses for thought-provoking ideas – demonstrating his commitment to knowledge and continual learning. Just looking at his online information has directed me to other podcasts and newsletters, to which I've also subscribed. (When an influencer recommends something, it's smart to follow!)

LinkedIn shows how this person has leveraged his success and profile to start his own global consultancy. He is a non-executive director to five companies and a start-up adviser and supporter. His profile states that he has won over 100 awards for his work in building brands and online capabilities and that he contributes regularly to an industry publication. He is currently employed as a CMO at another high-profile brand and he is the chairman of a marketing platform company.

There are always plenty of people who are ahead of us in the career journey who can provide inspiration and demonstrate success in action. Becoming a fan will give you the opportunity to see how people display the characteristics of success in different ways and may provide a model that could work for you.

2. Design your levers

In case you can't tell, I really don't want you to walk away from this book without taking any action. It's so easy to invest your time to read something, agree with the sentiment of the book and then walk away. I want this experience to be different for you. One way to do that is to design some levers – actions you can take to help you to become a deliberate digital marketer on an ongoing basis.

For me, I'm a planner and organisation fan. If I want to remember something, I use calendar reminders and forward planning. It means that I block out time in my calendar if I want to do something regularly, or I add recurring reminders into my task list. I also document my goals and break them into smaller tasks that I can add to my calendar and task list. If I am simply reminded at the right times of my desire and commitments, I can take steps forward.

The levers that work for you will be different to what works for me, so find the ways that work for your style and personality. You may not be able to incorporate regular time into your calendar in this way, so think about whether you can spend a week every six months or annually to batch-task your career progression instead. You might prefer to map out your plan and timelines using a whiteboard or a diary and written lists.

Whichever approach you take, you have an opportunity right now to identify some levers that will help you commit to progress. Please take a moment to decide what prompts will help you commit the time to do the work associated with improving yourself and your career.

3. Don't do it alone

Another great way to make a commitment to change is to do it with a buddy. Being accountable to someone will help both of you progress and provide the motivation you need. If you can think of someone in a similar role to you who is motivated and wants to get ahead, give them a copy of this book and ask them to be your accountability buddy. You can work through the steps together and have a regular check in to see how you are progressing in making change.

In the same way that a gym buddy keeps you getting up early, an accountability buddy can hold you to the goals you set. They can go to that event with you and make sure you turn up when you're having second thoughts – and once you are at the event, you can agree to meeting new people and following through afterwards. Together, you can motivate and encourage one another.

Be an inspiration

With all your new knowledge and the right motivation and levers in place, I have no doubt that you can make big changes to your effectiveness and job satisfaction and access better opportunities in your digital marketing career. If you follow the steps outlined, you can take the fast track to differentiate yourself from your peers and be the best digital marketer you can be. It's exciting, isn't it?

But once you are on the other side and basking in the joys of amplified results and a higher profile, make sure you remember the next generation of marketers coming behind you.

There will always be more people coming through the ranks who need help with learning and growing. Just like you, these people will be going through the motions, not yet kicking the goals they want. And you will be able to help.

Pay it forward

Never be afraid that helping another person may elevate them above you or negatively affect your career. No one can replicate or replace you: if you gave someone your exact map, they would still end up in a different place.

There is something special about helping others, as it allows you to share your experience and give back. Giving back could come in the form of being a mentor or simply helping with advice and direction. You might see a colleague struggling with big decisions and lend a willing ear or tell them about what you've learnt from this book. Maybe you can say yes to that invitation to speak at a small event with students and give those starting out a boost. Not only do these opportunities enable you to pay it forward but they also build relationships on different level, and who knows how that could play out in the future.

Remain approachable

Don't change who you are as a result of your success. There is nothing worse than seeing someone elevate in their profession and then become completely inaccessible and closed off. Yes, you may receive more emails and more requests, and this can be draining, but you will also receive more opportunities. If your emails start to get out of hand, get some help, organise them differently or outsource them – it's a step that many successful people need to take.

Commit to remaining approachable and continue to share. Don't always rush off after you present at an event; take a moment to continue your learning and to meet others in the room. Even once you have a great network, you can still benefit from building relationships. Answer that email, even if your response is brief. Take a moment to reply to the comments that people leave on your blog. Simply leaving a response will delight people.

There is no end

You can inspire others with your story, your success and the way you continue to follow the Deliberate Digital Marketer Framework. This isn't a one-off guide to success, something you can achieve and then forget. The characteristics in this framework will become a part of you and will guide how you work on an ongoing basis. There is no end to learning, to trying and to improving. You can never stop building relationships, amplifying your results or building your reputation. We are marketers – this is what we do.

Now, go and market yourself.

Next Steps

If you would like help implementing the suggestions in this book, visit the accompanying online resources. Take the 'Deliberate Digital Marketer Quiz' to see what stage you are at, or access PDF versions of the section checklists and discover my list of relevant industry events and resources.

Visit www.DeliberateDigitalMarketer.com

If you want to continue your learning, attend an Interactive Minds event or class at www.interactiveminds.com

You can do anything if you put your mind to it.

MY DAD

Acknowledgements

I'd like to thank my mum, Roslyn Francke. I couldn't do what I do without you as my biggest supporter, adviser and cheerleader. On top of that you have spent many, many hours looking after my kids and doing all types of domestic jobs so that I can work and do what I love. Thank you.

Thank you to Steve, Oliver, Ethan and Kiara. You are my reason for being and the sunshine in my life. It hasn't been easy trying to balance my ambitions and love of work with a young family (who interrupt me sometimes up to three times when writing just one sentence!) but having you here with me gives my life a purpose. Steven, thank you for your love, for sharing your ambition and business input, and for your support and belief in what I do.

My dad has been a constant champion of hard work and achievement, so thank you to my dad, Malcolm Francke, for making that part of who I am too. My brother has always been there to challenge me, which only makes me try harder. As Mum always used to say, 'If you can survive a brother you can survive anything!' So Martin, I can thank you for my resilience! Thank you also to David, Dianne and my extended family for your interest in what I do and for your love.

There are many people who have helped me to bring this book to life with their experiences, input and advice. Thank you all for being excited about what I've been doing and supporting the vision.

Specifically, I'd like to thank all the people I interviewed for this book: Laura Campbell, Ronsley Vaz, David Gram, Jeremiah Andrick, Wes Finley, Georgia Ball, Milan Narayan, Cary Brown, Lola Wheller, Carla North, Louise Flynn, Holly Tattersall and Nathan McKean.

Thank you to my advisory panel, Rob Hudson, Han te Riele, Emma Croston and Naina D'Souza, for your ongoing input over the years, which has helped shape many events, and in turn my business.

To those I have partnered with in business, Warren Barry and Jen Story, you both taught me so much. Sarah Mak, thank you for your advice and friendship. Brendt Sheen, I find our catch-ups so valuable. A big thank you to Dave Eddy for offering to read a draft and being the first person I was brave enough to show this book to. I appreciate your invaluable guidance and enthusiastic support. Thank you to the Dent team and wider community too – your education and network have been vital to my business.

To my first mentor, Sarina Russo, I learnt a lot from being around you as a child and hearing your vision through my mum, who spent twenty years working for you. Your phrases, 'Fake it till you make it' and 'I'll see you at the top', have stuck with me. I learnt many business basics (including typing!) by spending school holidays helping in the office. Thank you for helping to shape my ambitious nature.

Thank you to all the other people who have contributed to what I'm doing and helped define the direction I've taken. To my friends who put up with me always taking on a little more than I should – Benji, Cody, Ben, Michelle, Gerrod, Kristy, Melanie, Janelle, Micah, Sarah, Bec, Beck, Nicole, Julia, Carley and your partners and families – I love hanging out with you in my downtime.

Thank you to my team who have helped me to bring my ideas to life and support my ambitious goals: Georgia Ball, Amber Dermoudy, Chris Philips, Lisa Renneisen, Nadine Zrinzo, Linh Diep, Colleen Lawes and Samantha Horton.

Finally, I'd like to give a special mention to all those people who have attended an event I have run over the last nine years. I have learnt so much from the conversations, the shared lessons and from your acquaintance. Thank you for your support – and for being the inspiration behind this book.

To achieve great things, two things are needed: a plan, and not quite enough time.

Leonard Bernstein

About Louisa Dahl

Louisa has always had an ambitious streak. She started selling bags of 'fertiliser' to neighbours when she was seven, and has since gone on to start three businesses.

After completing a degree in business, majoring in marketing, Louisa worked as a digital marketer for almost ten years before combining her love of business with her digital marketing experience to create her company, Interactive Minds. Now, nine years on, Interactive Minds provides events, training and resources to digital marketers around Australia.

Achievement has always been important to Louisa, whether it was working her way to the top position in a part-time job, positioning herself for promotion in her career or investing in continual learning to grow and achieve more. She hopes this book will help others to achieve a successful and fulfilling career, too.

If you want to explore how Interactive Minds helps digital marketers to stay up-to-date and achieve results, visit www.interactiveminds.com

Find out more about Louisa at www.louisadahl.com

www.ingramcontent.com/pod-product-compliance
Lightning Source LLC
Chambersburg PA
CBHW060312220326
41598CB00027B/4306